MAD
ABOUT SPORTS

Written by Frank Jacobs

Illustrated by Bob Clarke

Edited by Albert B. Feldstein

WARNER BOOKS

A Warner Communications Company

WARNER BOOKS EDITION

Copyright © 1977 by Frank Jacobs, Robert J. Clarke
and E.C. Publications, Inc.

ISBN 0-446-76689-5

This Warner Books Edition is published by
arrangement with E.C. Publications, Inc.

Warner Books, Inc., 75 Rockefeller Plaza, New York, N.Y. 10019

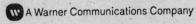 A Warner Communications Company

Printed in the United States of America

Not associated with Warner Press, Inc. of Anderson, Indiana

10   9   8   7   6   5   4   3   2   1

CONTENTS

THE SPORTS FANATIC

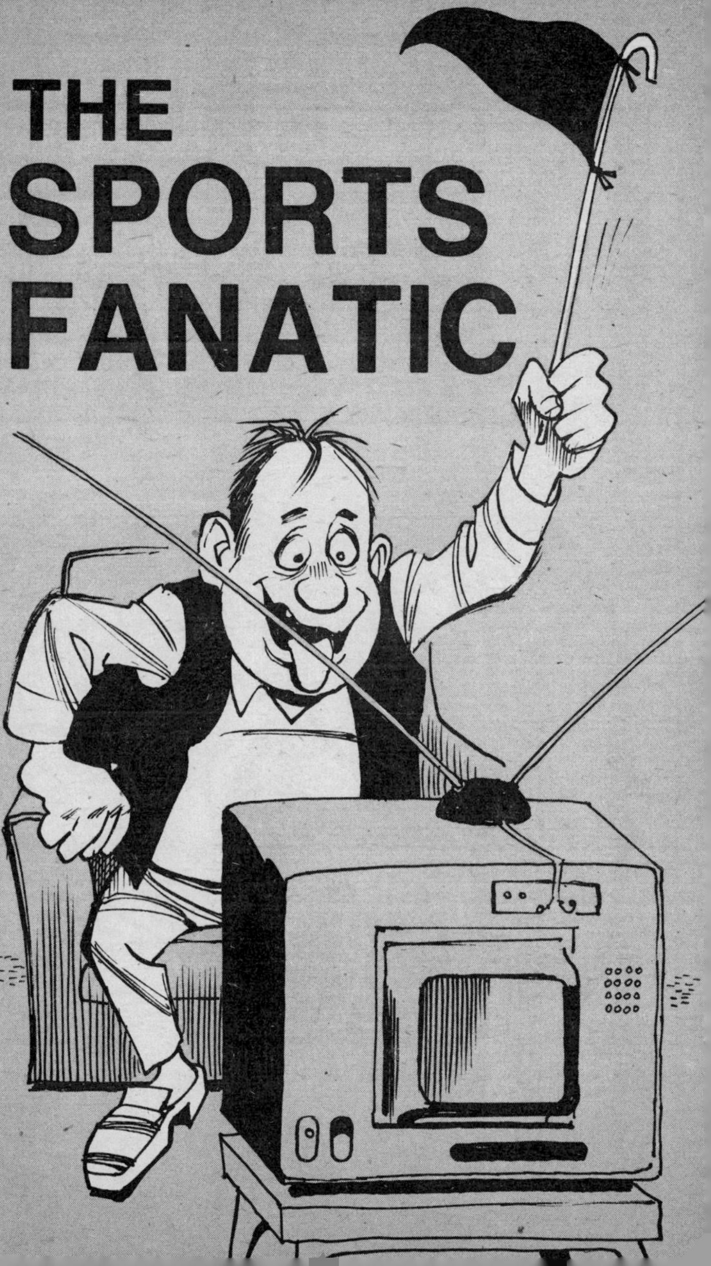

Meet Charlie, the Sports Fanatic. He's just like you and me–with one big difference. He lives, eats, sleeps and breathes Sports.

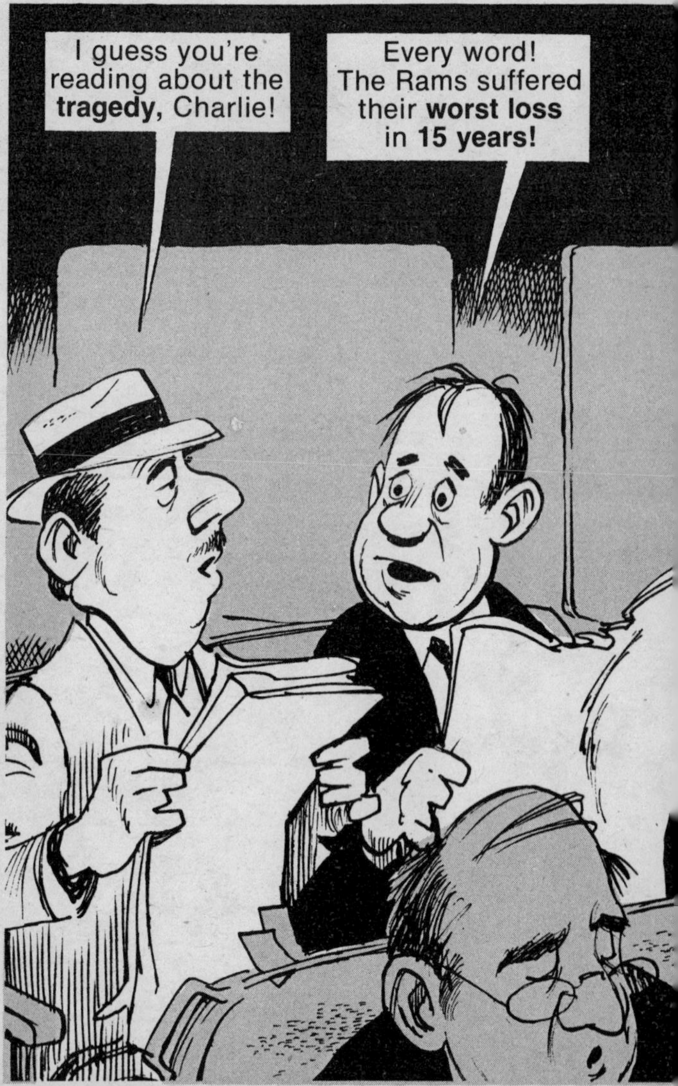

I guess you're reading about the **tragedy,** Charlie!
Every word! The Rams suffered their **worst loss** in **15 years!**

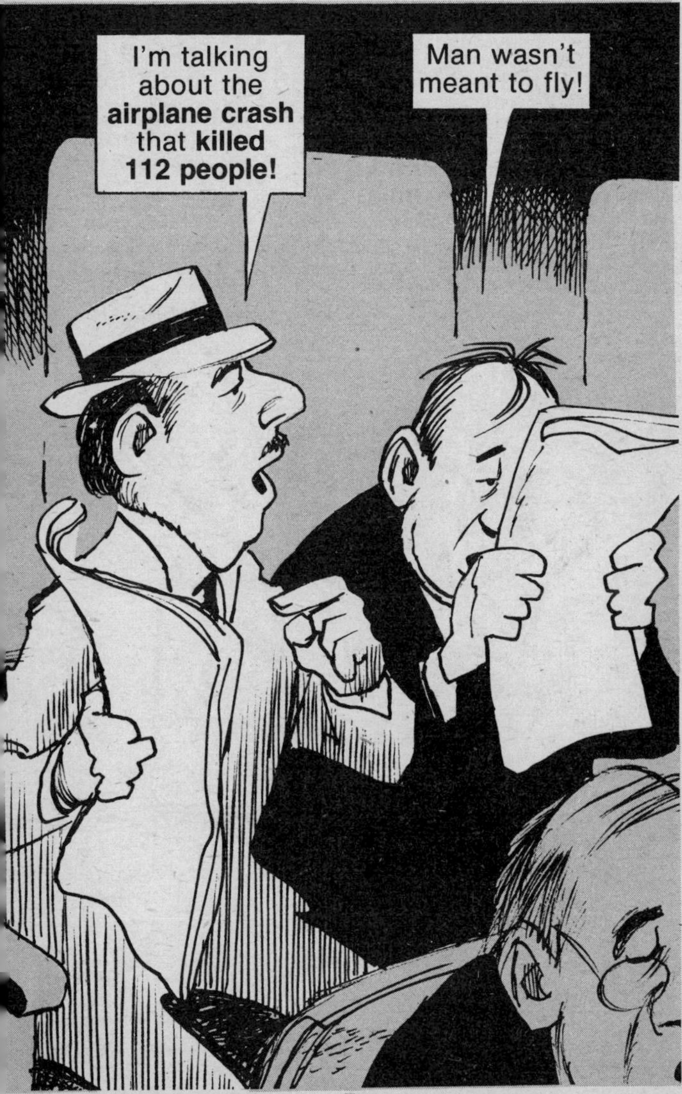
I'm talking about the **airplane crash** that **killed 112 people!**
Man wasn't meant to fly!

The Sports Fanatic isn't a bum. He has a job and provides for his family. But he never confuses his career with life's real goals.

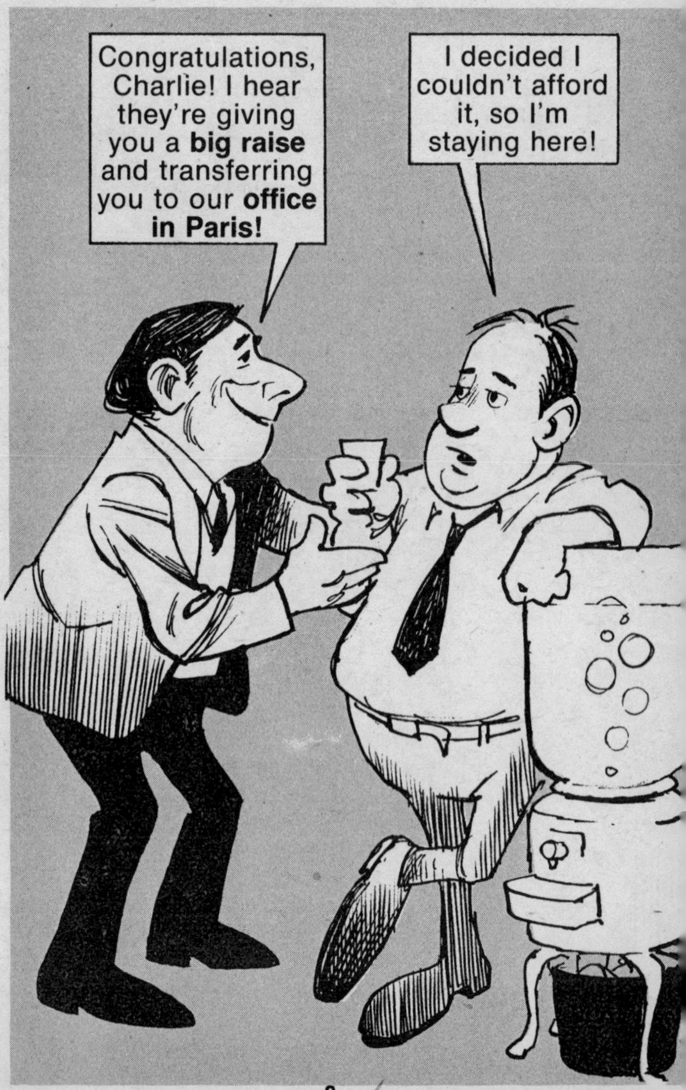
Congratulations, Charlie! I hear they're giving you a **big raise** and transferring you to our **office in Paris!**
I decided I couldn't afford it, so I'm staying here!

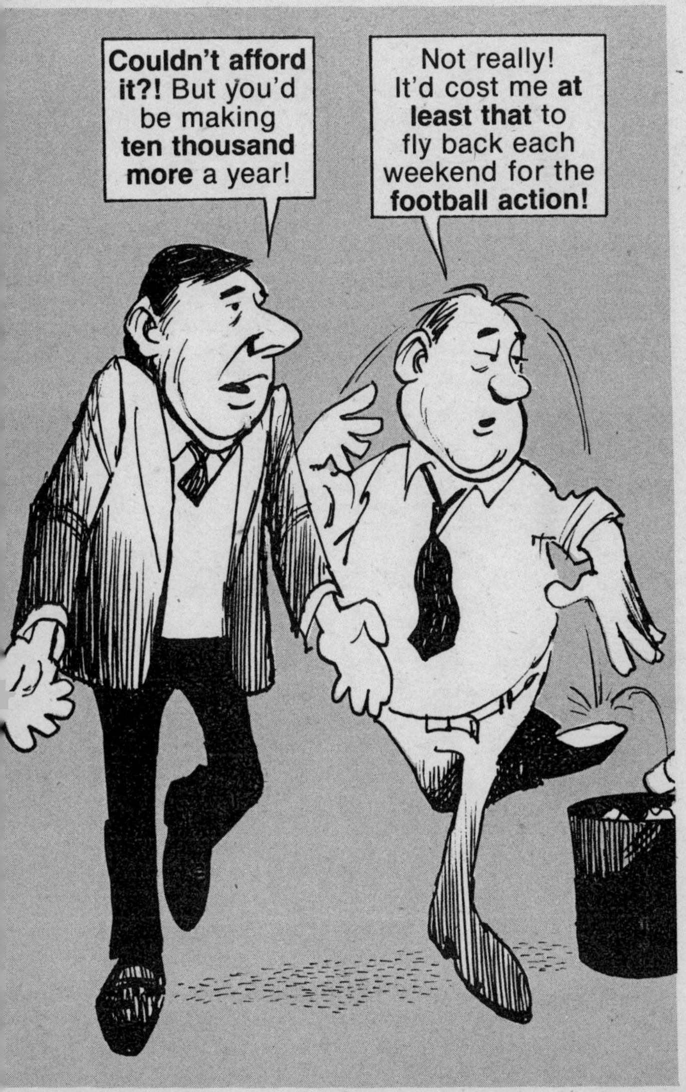
Couldn't afford it?! But you'd be making ten thousand more a year!
Not really! It'd cost me at least that to fly back each weekend for the football action!

At home the Sports Fanatic seems different from other men. This requires a great deal of understanding from the rest of his family.

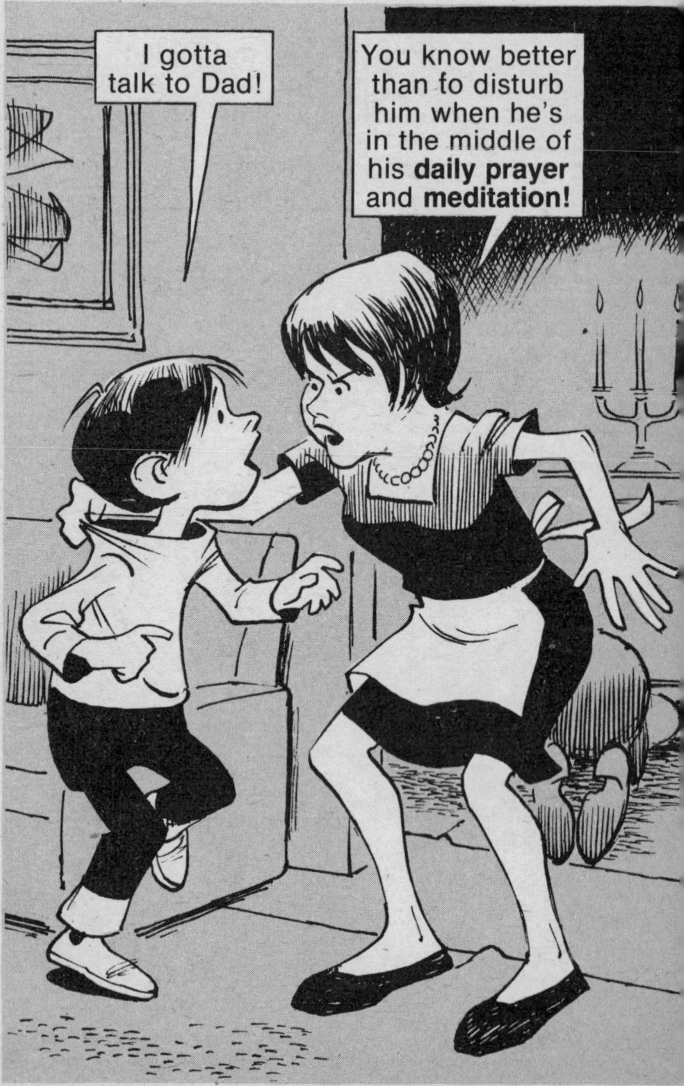
I gotta talk to Dad!
You know better than to disturb him when he's in the middle of his **daily prayer** and **meditation!**

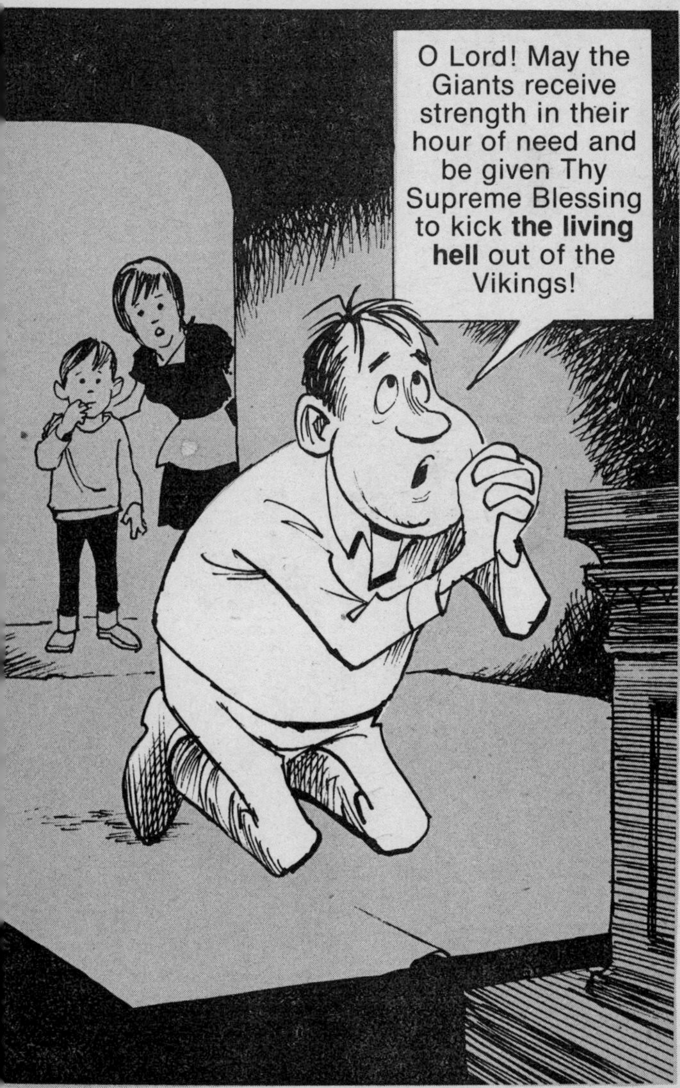
O Lord! May the Giants receive strength in their hour of need and be given Thy Supreme Blessing to kick **the living hell** out of the Vikings!

The Sports Fanatic likes other people and enjoys socializing, just so long as it takes place at a time that he considers convenient.

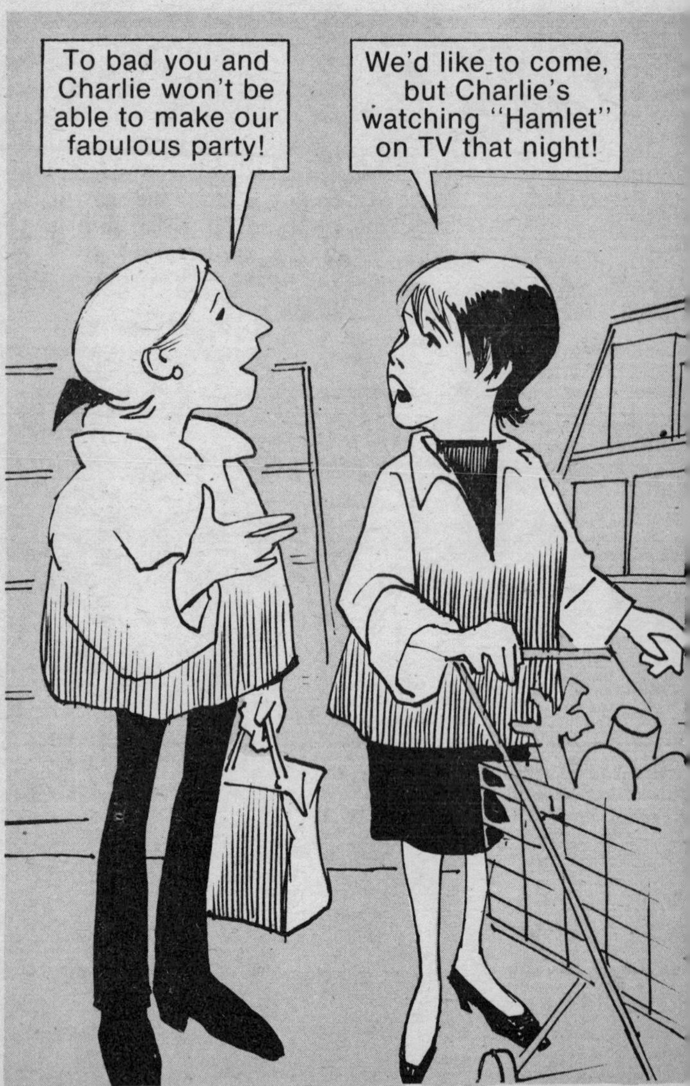
To bad you and Charlie won't be able to make our fabulous party!
We'd like to come, but Charlie's watching "Hamlet" on TV that night!

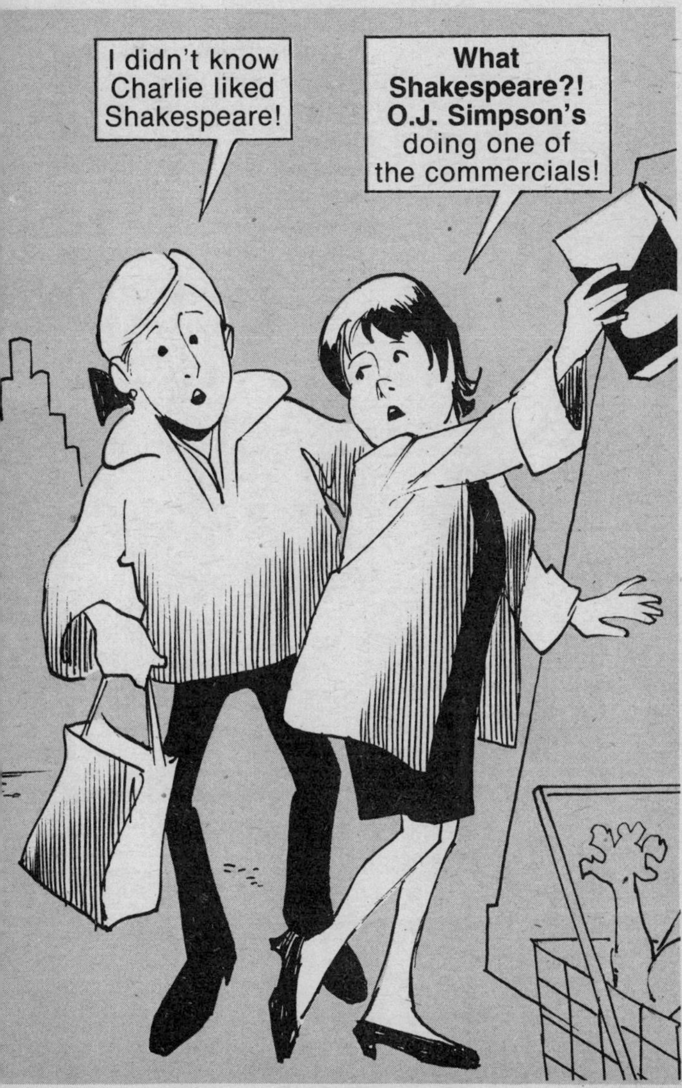
I didn't know Charlie liked Shakespeare!
What Shakespeare?! O.J. Simpson's doing one of the commercials!

The wife of the Sports Fanatic is a special sort of woman. She has to be. But there are those moments when even she loses her patience.

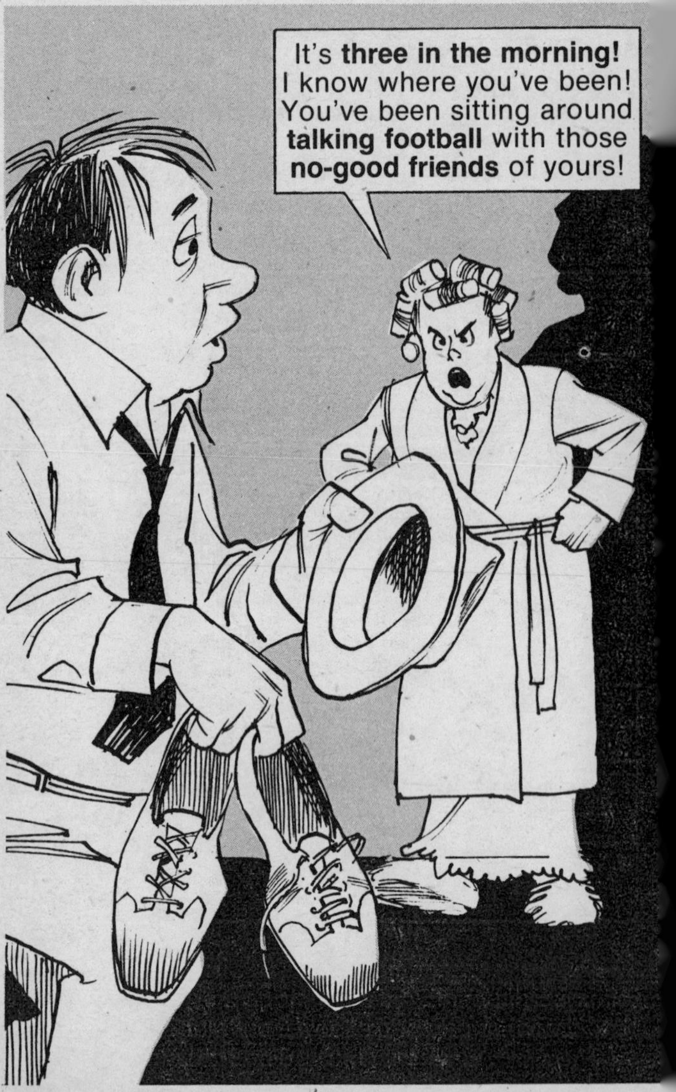
It's **three in the morning!** I know where you've been! You've been sitting around **talking football** with those **no-good friends** of yours!

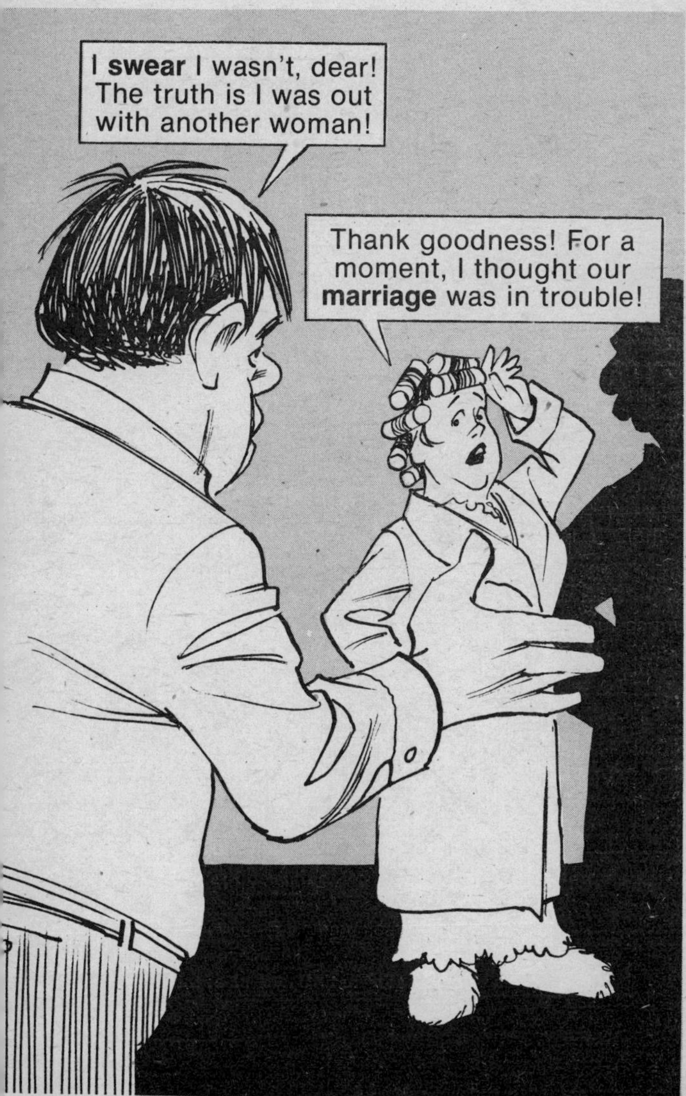
I **swear** I wasn't, dear! The truth is I was out with another woman!
Thank goodness! For a moment, I thought our **marriage** was in trouble!

Sometimes, in fact, the Sports Fanatic's wife loses her cool completely. When this happens, she can't control her temper and turns violent.

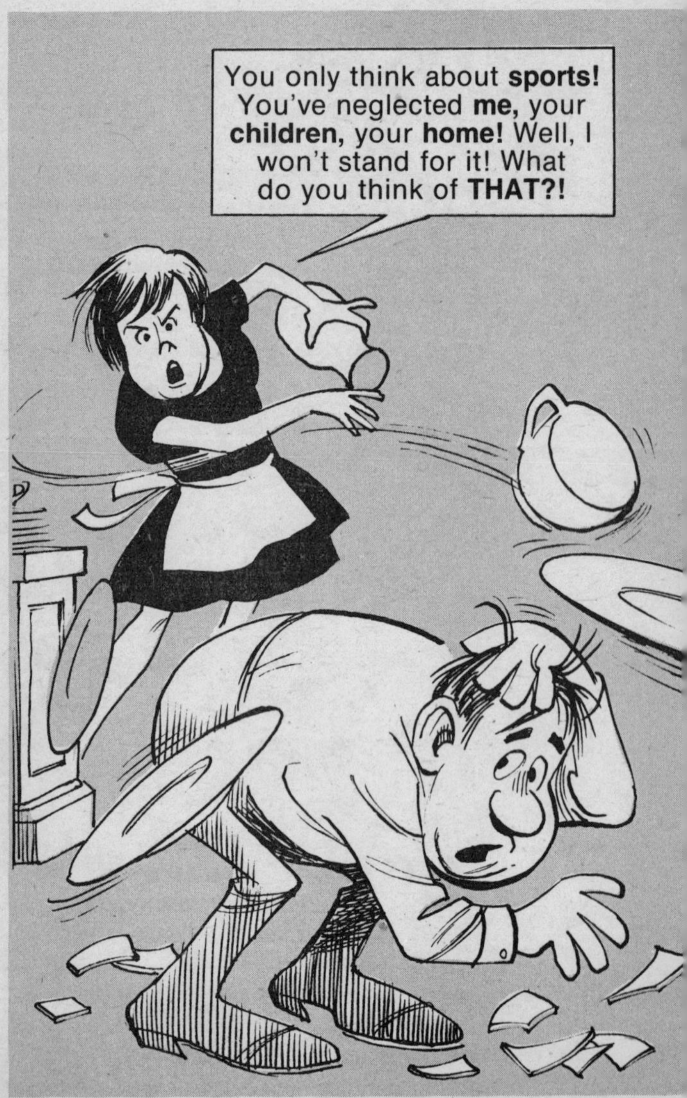
You only think about **sports!** You've neglected **me,** your **children,** your **home!** Well, I won't stand for it! What do you think of **THAT?!**

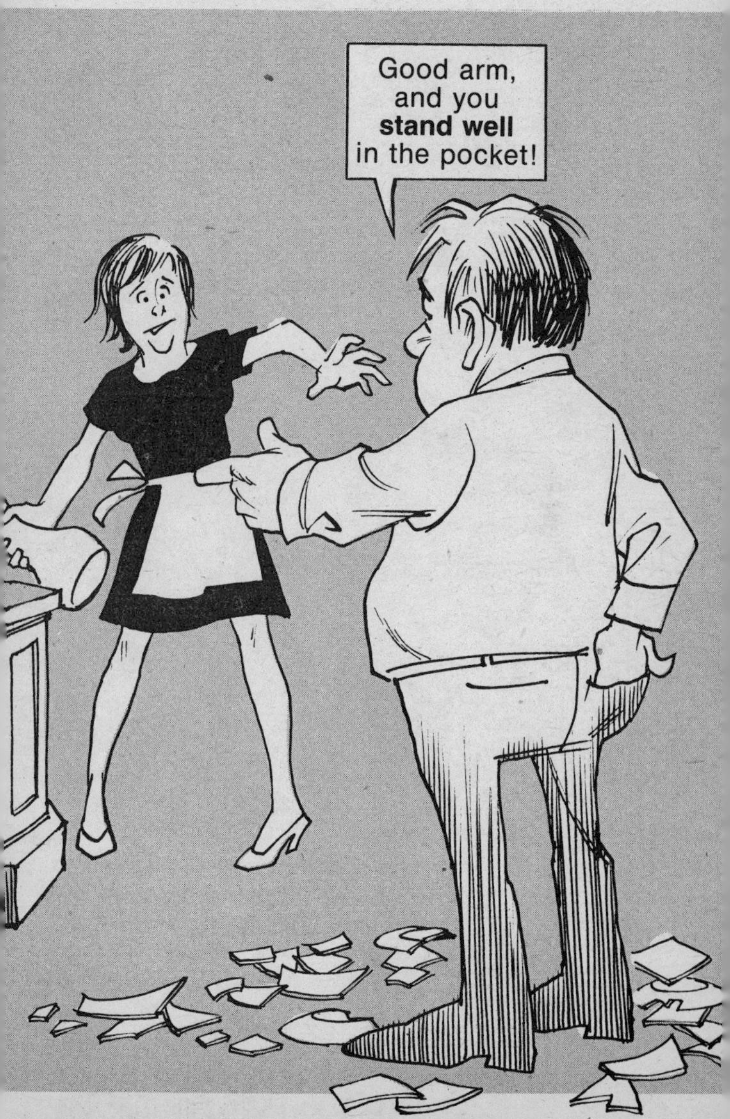
Good arm, and you **stand well** in the pocket!

Once in a while, it's the Sports Fanatic who loses his temper. After such outbursts, he may find himself forced to account for his actions!

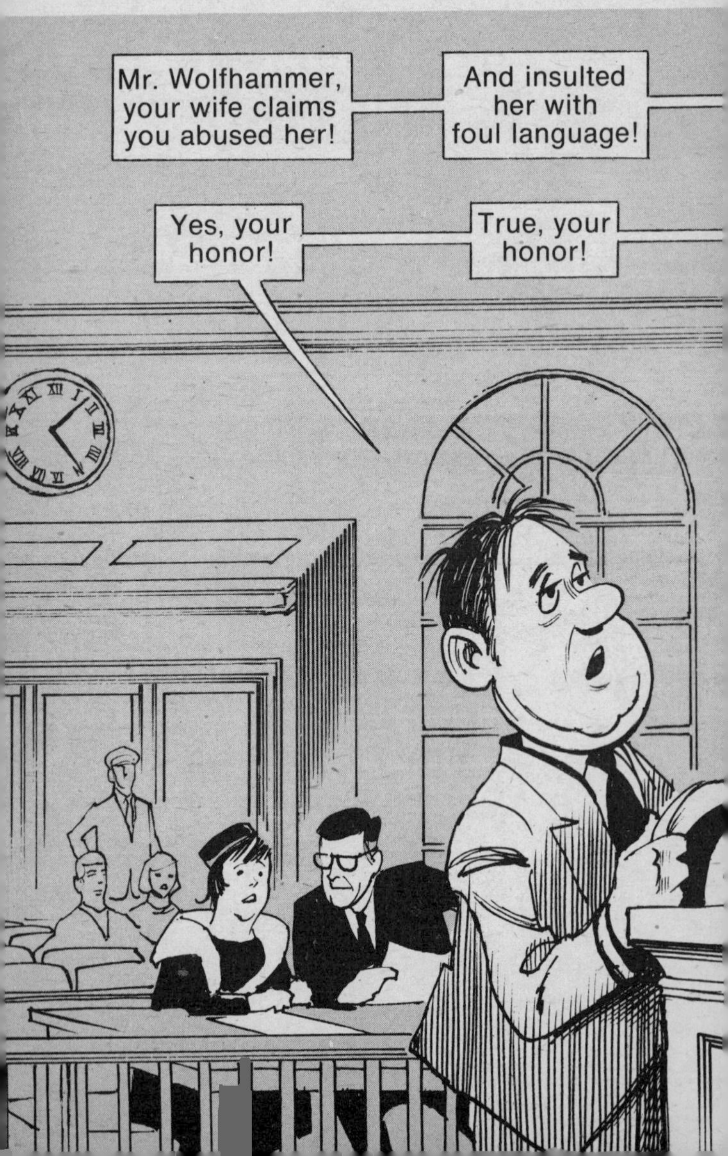

Mr. Wolfhammer, your wife claims you abused her!
And insulted her with foul language!
Yes, your honor!
True, your honor!

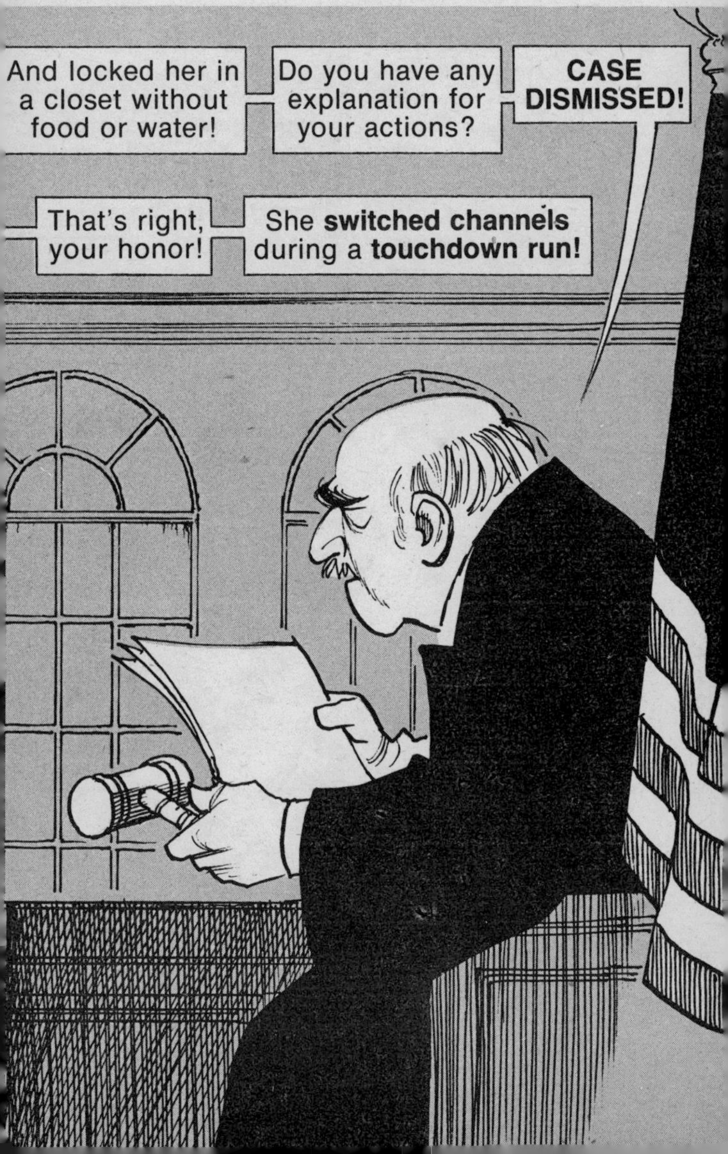
And locked her in a closet without food or water!
Do you have any explanation for your actions?
CASE DISMISSED!
That's right, your honor!
She switched channels during a touchdown run!

But basically the Sports Fanatic is a good sort, and even though he can't change his ways; he does his best to patch things up and make amends!

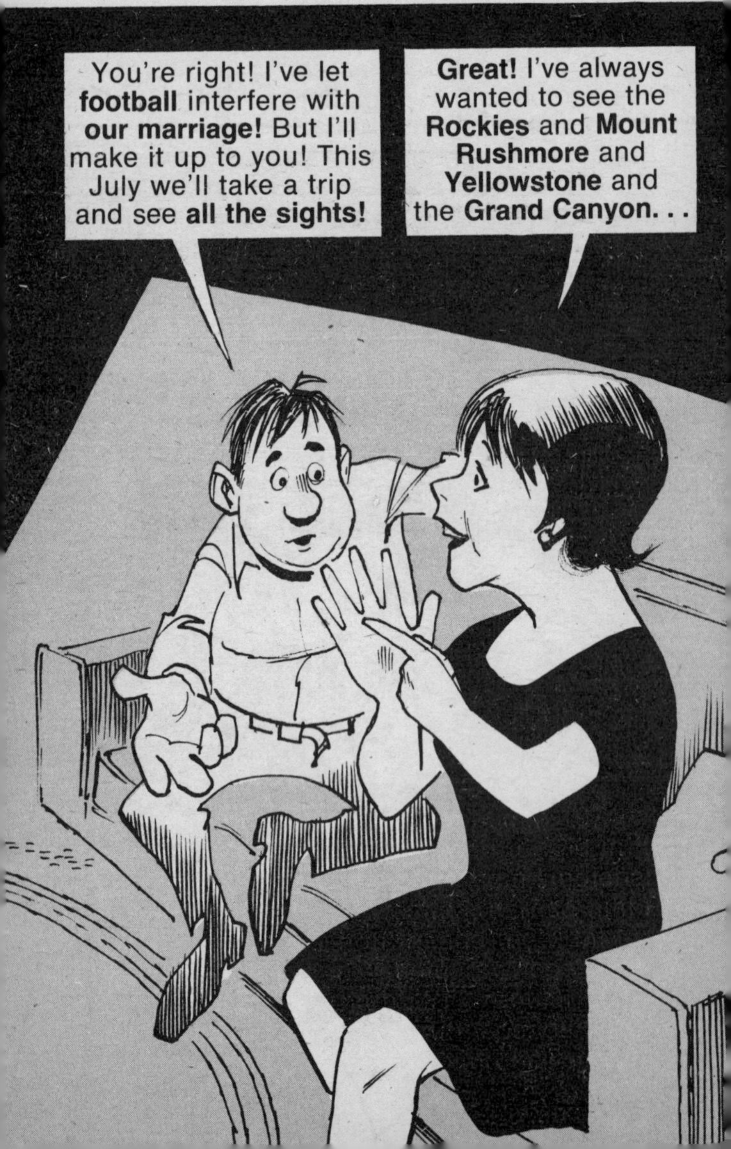
You're right! I've let **football** interfere with **our marriage!** But I'll make it up to you! This July we'll take a trip and see **all the sights!**
Great! I've always wanted to see the **Rockies** and **Mount Rushmore** and **Yellowstone** and the **Grand Canyon. . .**

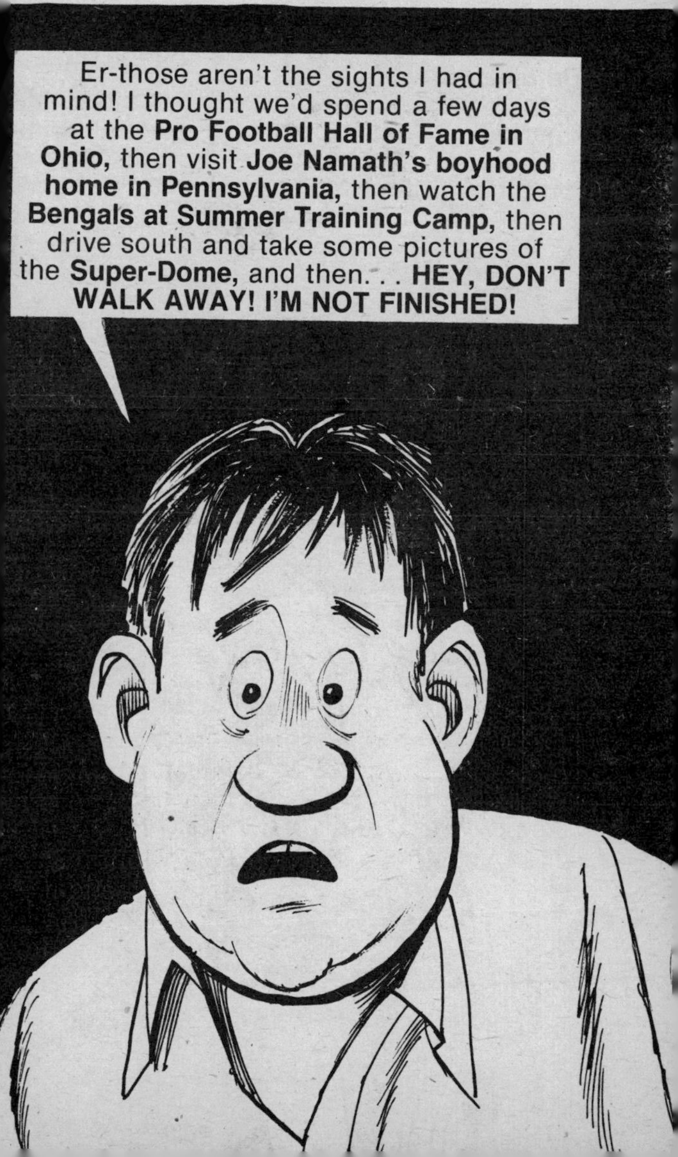
Er-those aren't the sights I had in mind! I thought we'd spend a few days at the **Pro Football Hall of Fame in Ohio,** then visit **Joe Namath's boyhood home in Pennsylvania,** then watch the **Bengals at Summer Training Camp,** then drive south and take some pictures of the **Super-Dome,** and then. . . **HEY, DON'T WALK AWAY! I'M NOT FINISHED!**

Don't think the Sports Fanatic is only a creature of touchdowns and field goals! He's a deeply emotional human being like all of us.

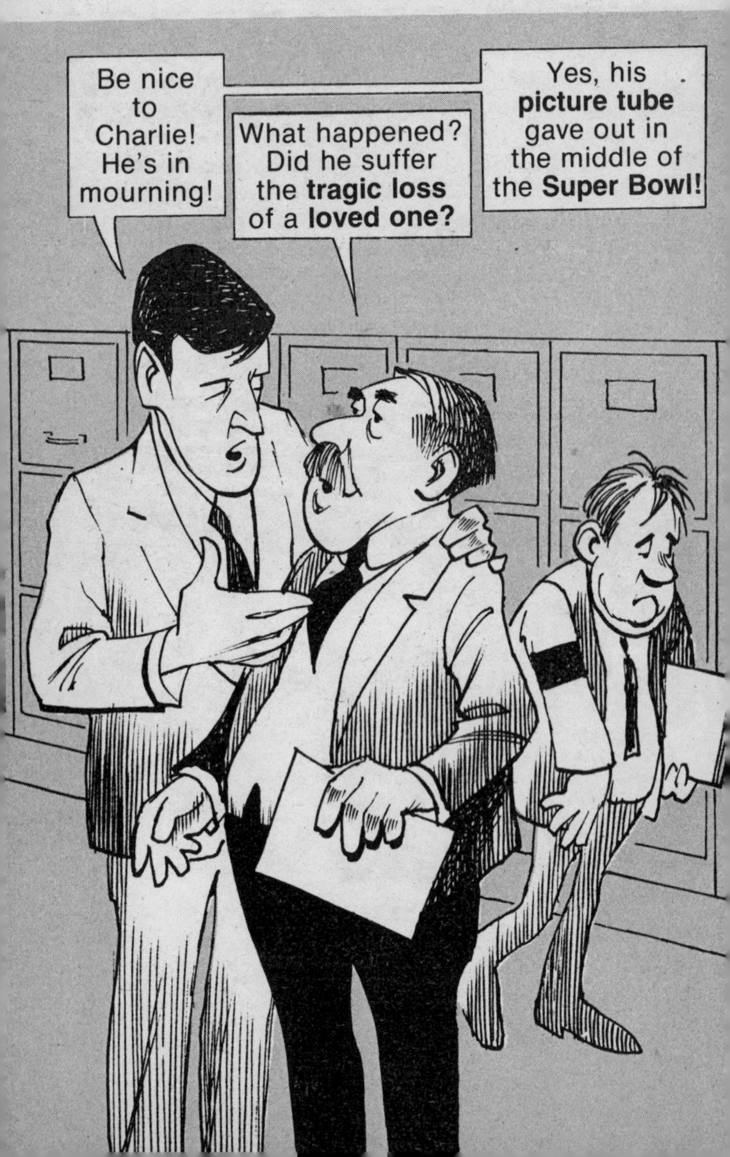

Be nice to Charlie! He's in mourning!
What happened? Did he suffer the **tragic loss** of a **loved one?**
Yes, his **picture tube** gave out in the middle of the **Super Bowl!**

And he's also a creature of flesh and bone, who can fall ill like anyone else, although, to be sure, he needs a special kind of care.

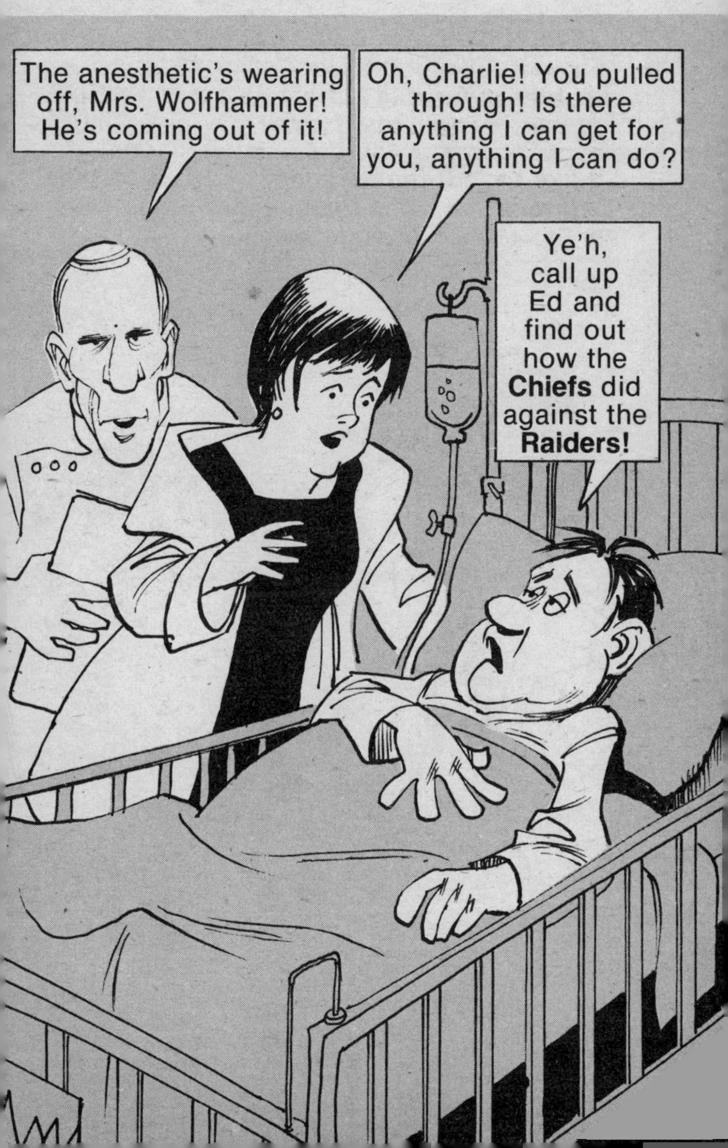
The anesthetic's wearing off, Mrs. Wolfhammer! He's coming out of it!
Oh, Charlie! You pulled through! Is there anything I can get for you, anything I can do?
Ye'h, call up Ed and find out how the **Chiefs** did against the **Raiders!**

Death eventually comes to the Sports Fanatic, and he enters that Great End Zone in the Sky. He is mourned by his family and his friends.

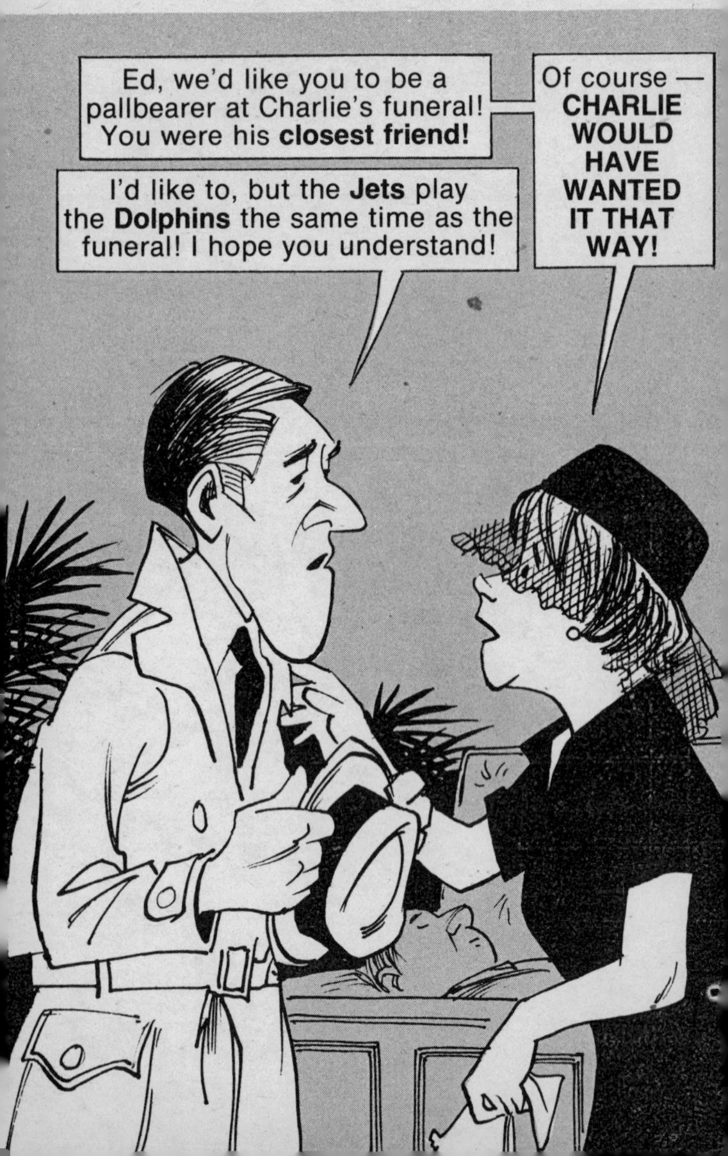
Ed, we'd like you to be a pallbearer at Charlie's funeral! You were his **closest friend!**
I'd like to, but the **Jets** play the **Dolphins** the same time as the funeral! I hope you understand!
Of course — **CHARLIE WOULD HAVE WANTED IT THAT WAY!**

THE LOSERS

What they say

in public & in private

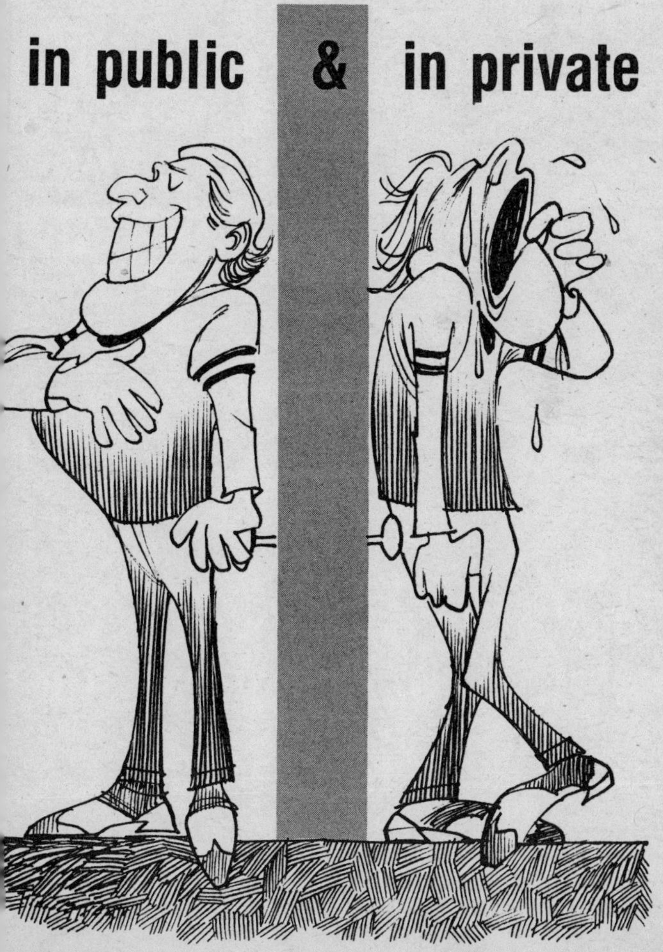

The Losing Football Coach

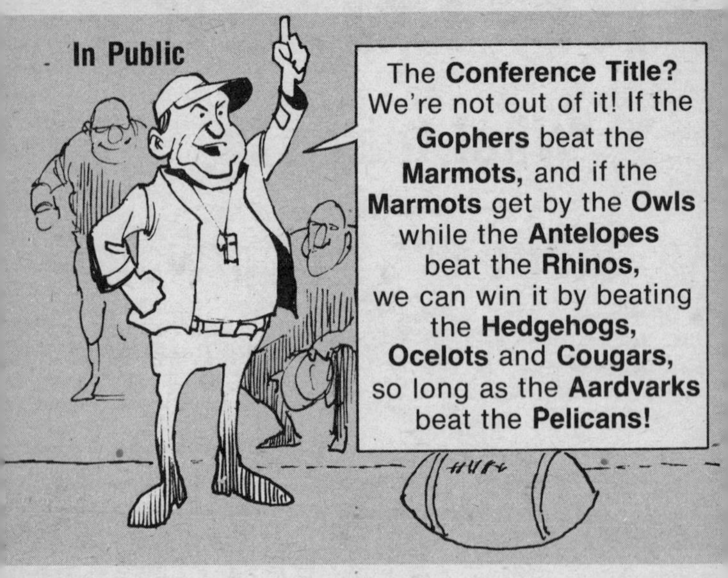
In Public
The **Conference Title?** We're not out of it! If the **Gophers** beat the **Marmots,** and if the **Marmots** get by the **Owls** while the **Antelopes** beat the **Rhinos,** we can win it by beating the **Hedgehogs, Ocelots** and **Cougars,** so long as the **Aardvarks** beat the **Pelicans!**

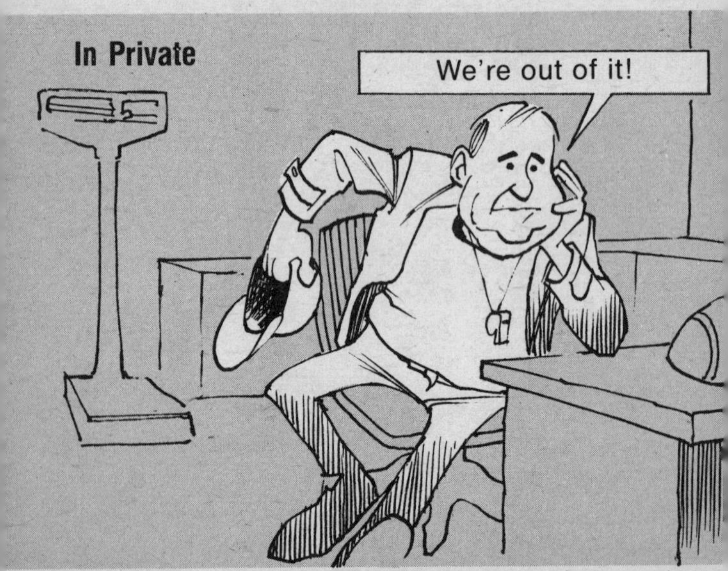
In Private
We're out of it!

The Losing Hockey Coach

In Public

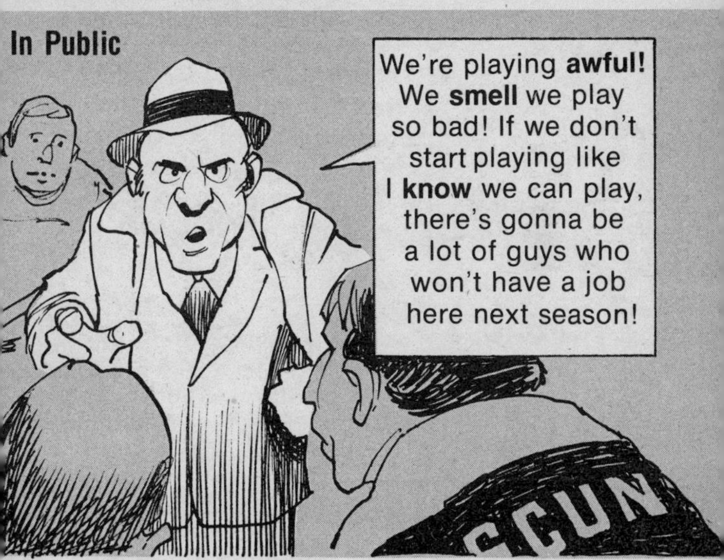
We're playing **awful!** We **smell** we play so bad! If we don't start playing like I **know** we can play, there's gonna be a lot of guys who won't have a job here next season!
CCUN

In Private

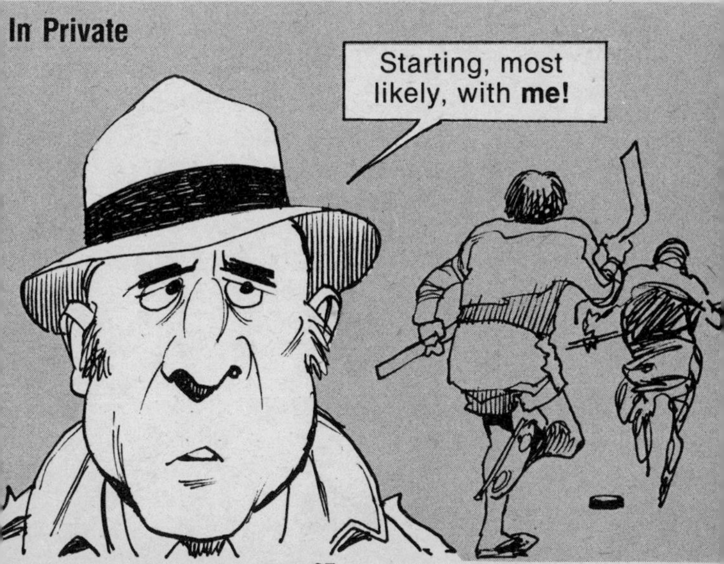
Starting, most likely, with **me!**

The Losing Basketball Coach

In Public

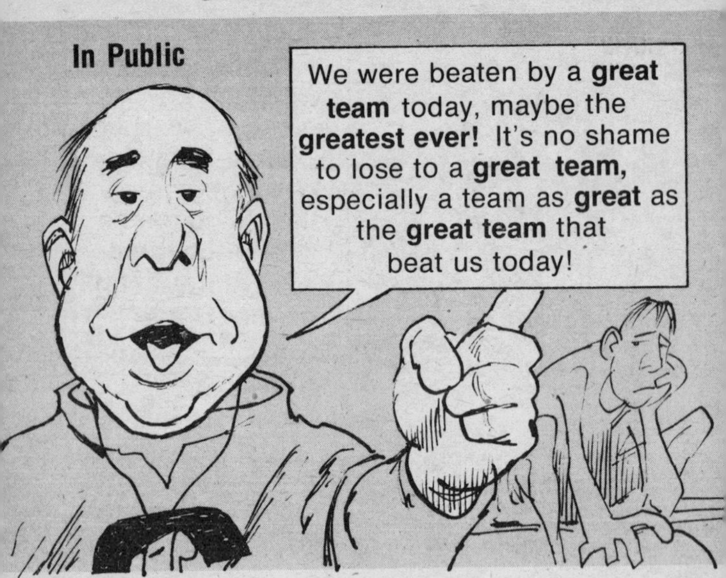
We were beaten by a **great team** today, maybe the **greatest ever!** It's no shame to lose to a **great team,** especially a team as **great** as the **great team** that beat us today!

In Private

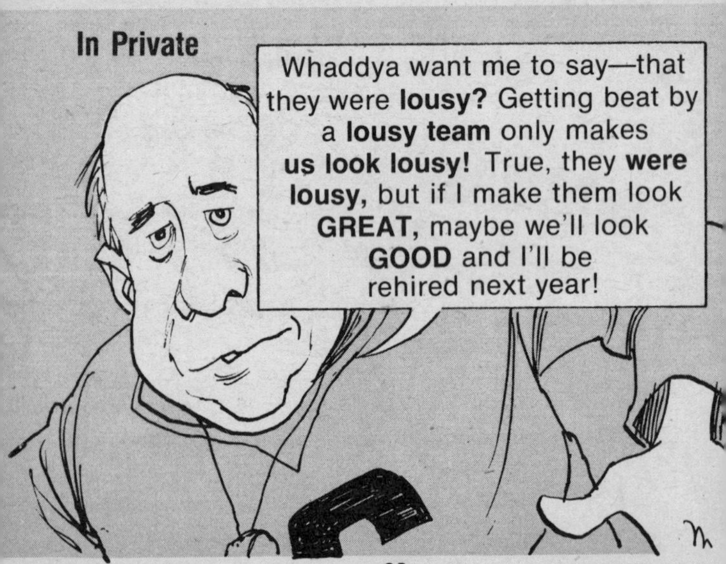
Whaddya want me to say—that they were **lousy?** Getting beat by a **lousy team** only makes **us look lousy!** True, they **were lousy,** but if I make them look **GREAT,** maybe we'll look **GOOD** and I'll be rehired next year!

The Losing Little League Coach

In Public

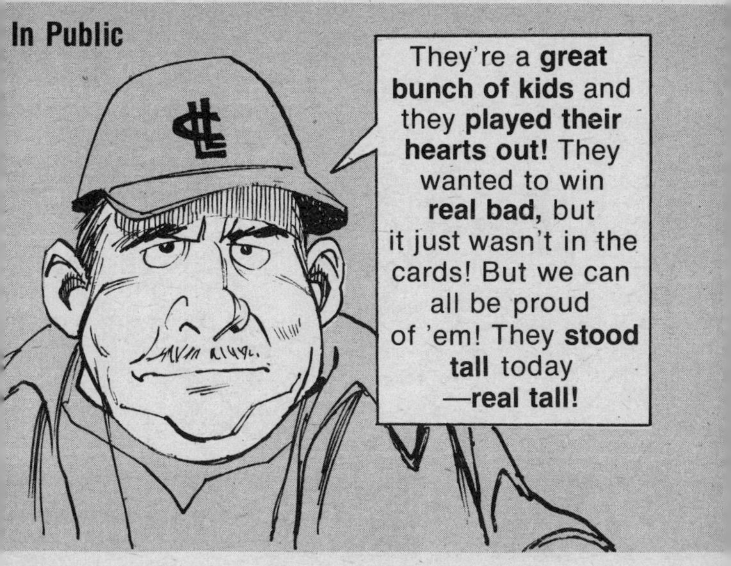
They're a **great bunch of kids** and they **played their hearts out!** They wanted to win **real bad,** but it just wasn't in the cards! But we can all be proud of 'em! They **stood tall** today —**real tall!**

In Private

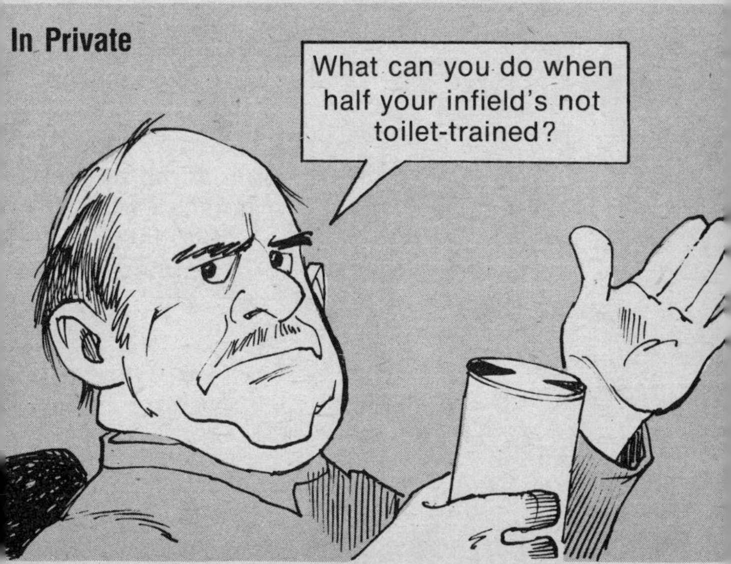
What can you do when half your infield's not toilet-trained?

The Losing Jockey

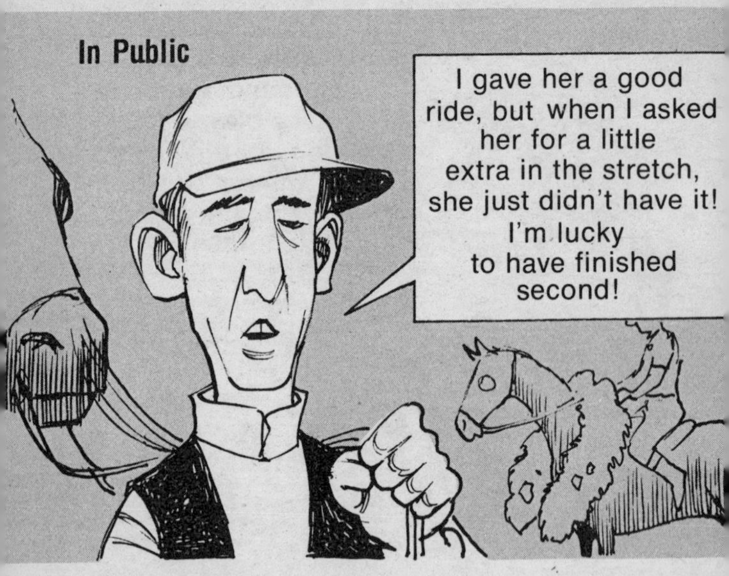
In Public
I gave her a good ride, but when I asked her for a little extra in the stretch, she just didn't have it! I'm lucky to have finished second!

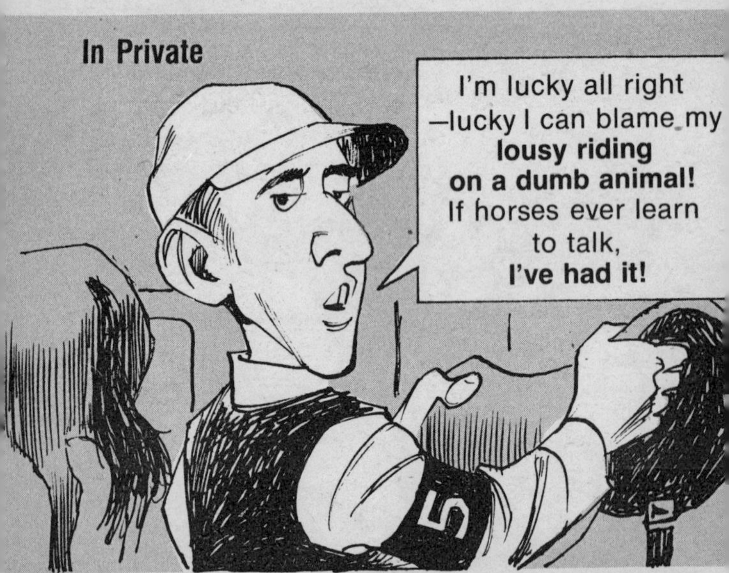
In Private
I'm lucky all right —lucky I can blame my **lousy riding on a dumb animal!** If horses ever learn to talk, **I've had it!**
5

The Losing Chess Player

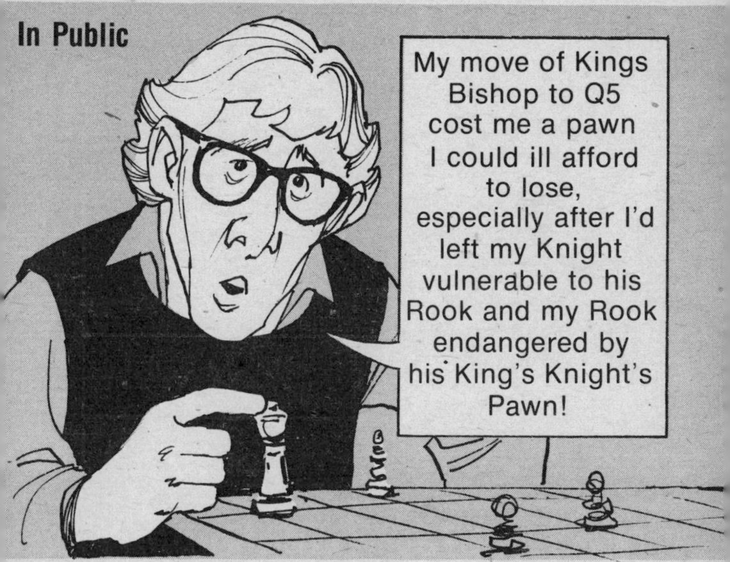
In Public
My move of Kings Bishop to Q5 cost me a pawn I could ill afford to lose, especially after I'd left my Knight vulnerable to his Rook and my Rook endangered by his King's Knight's Pawn!

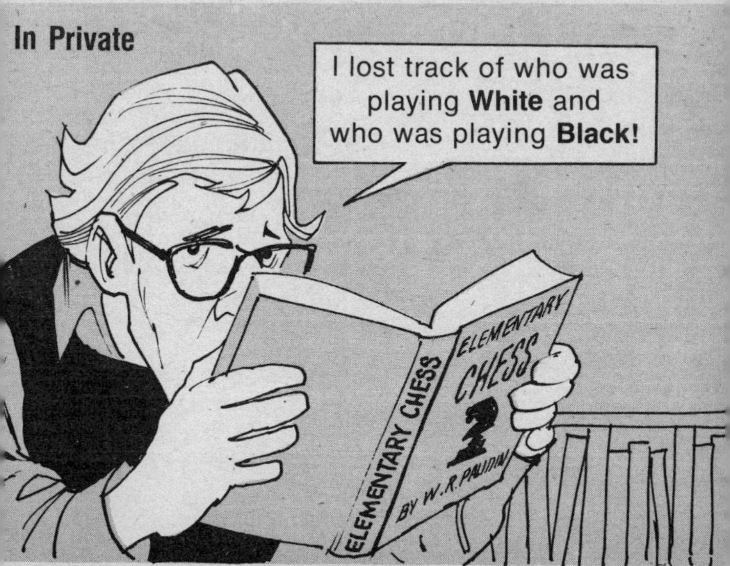
In Private
I lost track of who was playing **White** and who was playing **Black!**
ELEMENTARY CHESS
ELEMENTARY CHESS
BY W.R. PAUDIN

SPORTS CLOSE-UPS

Fan at Baseball Game Waiting to Catch Foul Ball

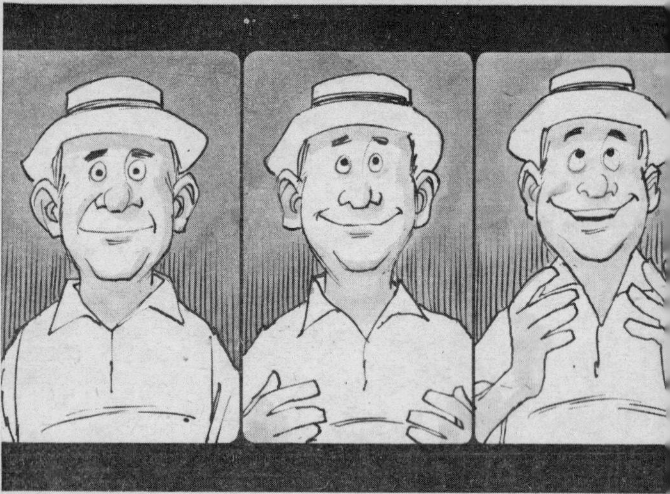

Spectator with Allergy Watching Crucial Golf Putt

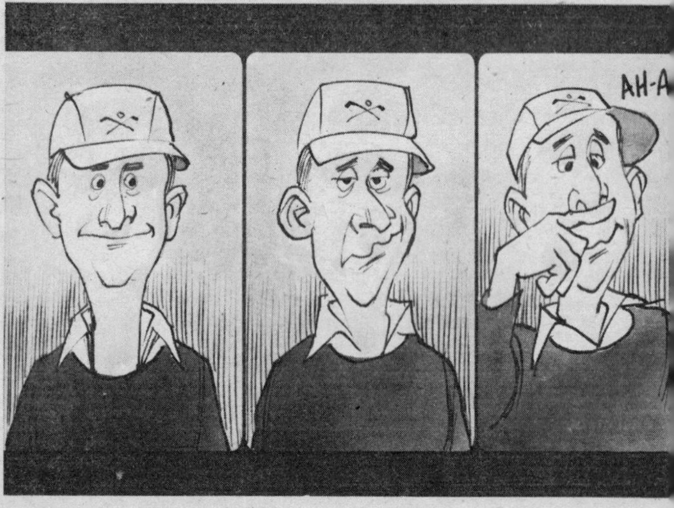
AH-A

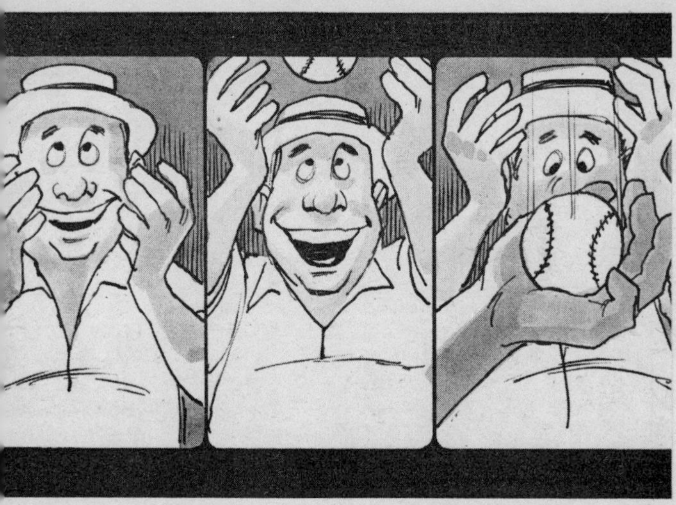

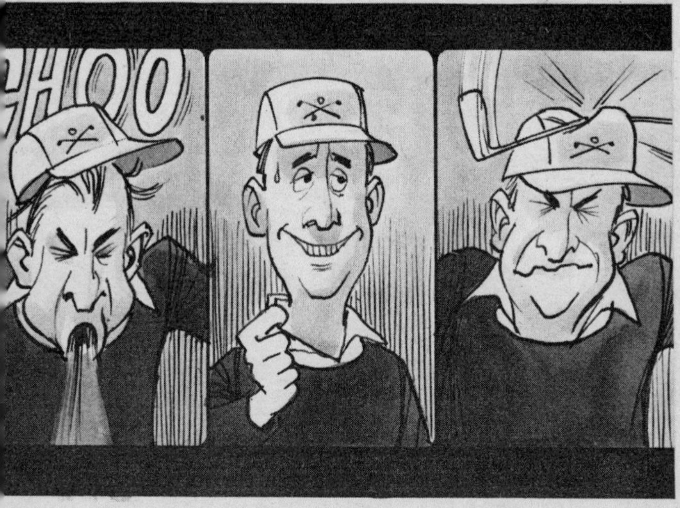
HOO

Fan Watching Hockey Puck Sail Over Glass into Crowd

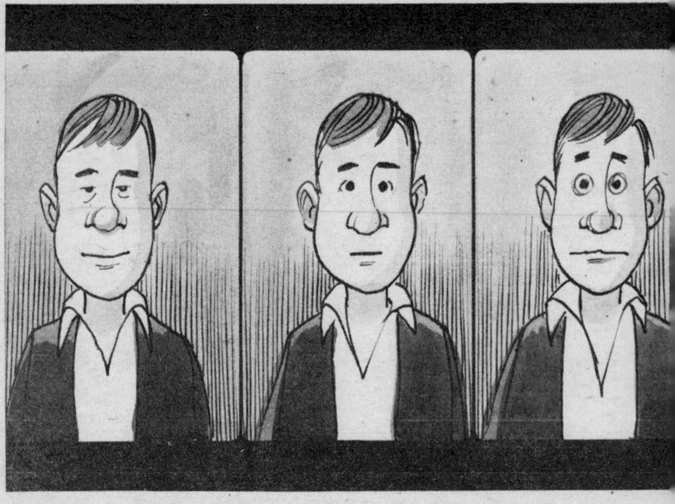

Fan Watching Fullback Gain 35 Yards

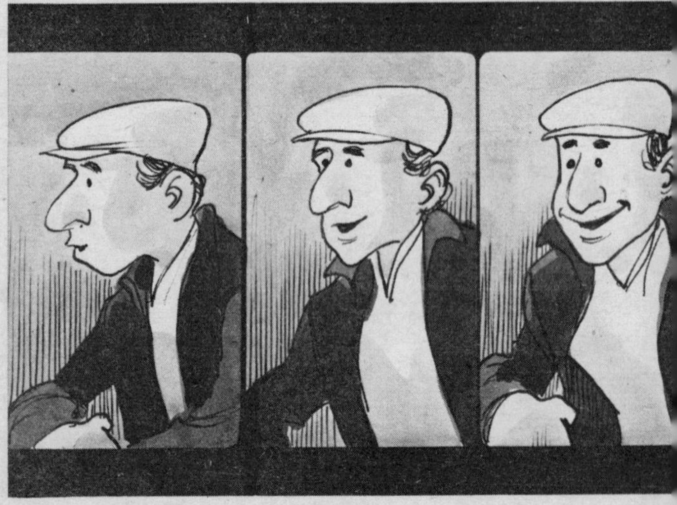

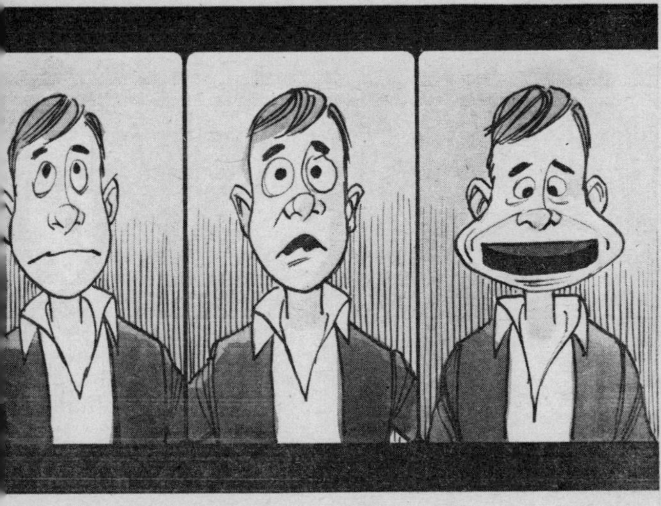

Then Meet 4 Tacklers

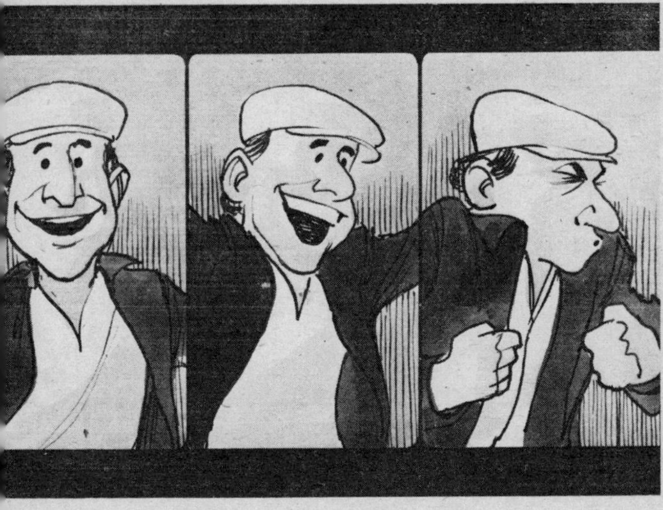

Fan Annoyed His Team is Behind 49 to 0 in First Half

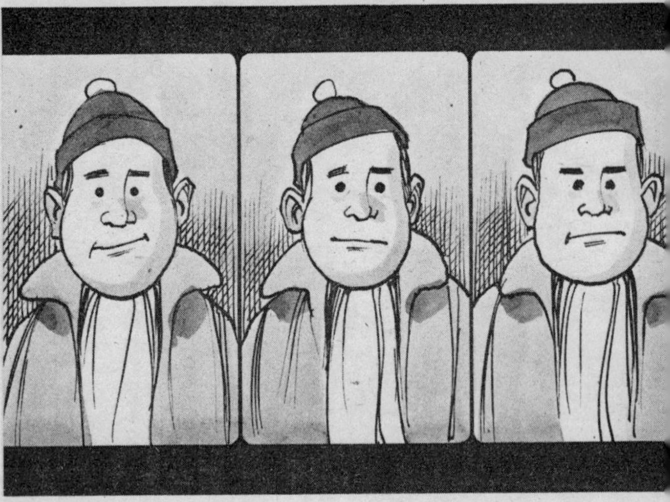

Fan Not Caring His Team is Behind 49 to 0 in First Half

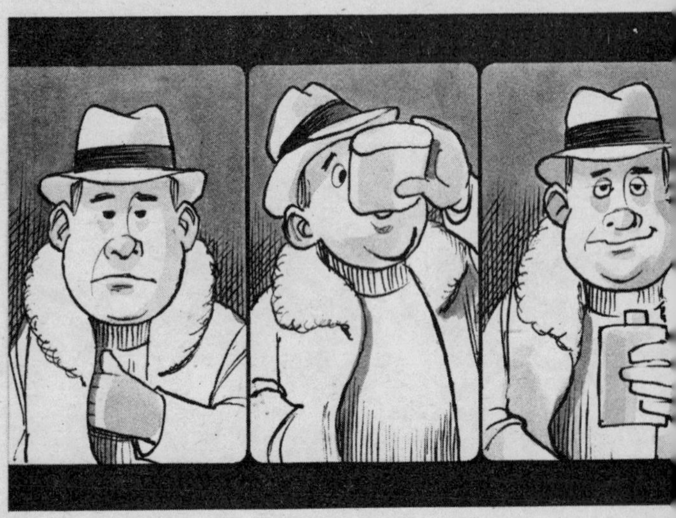

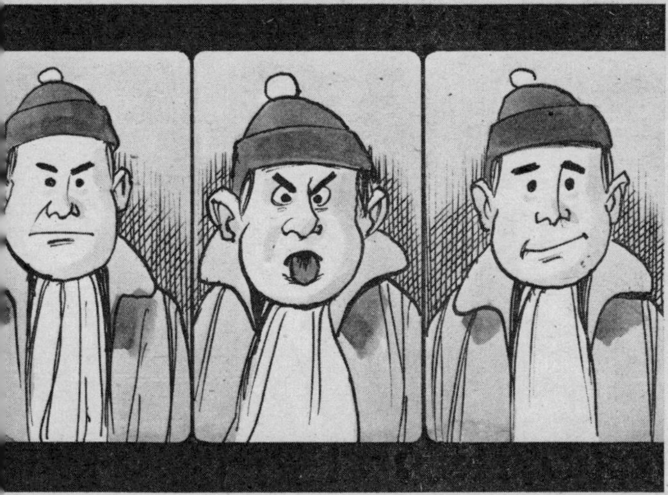

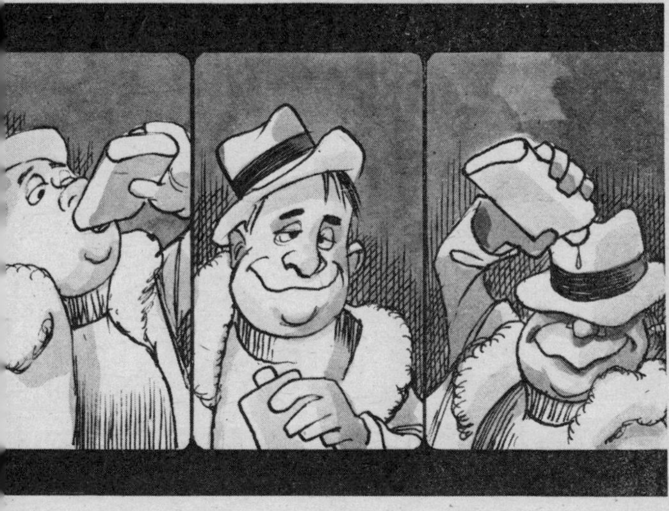

Tourist Watching Especially Gruesome Bullfight

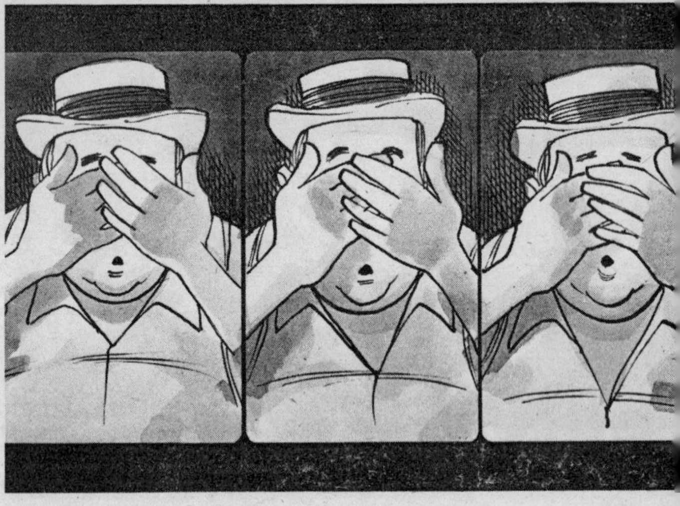

Fan Caught Up in Spirit of Viciously Fought Boxing Match

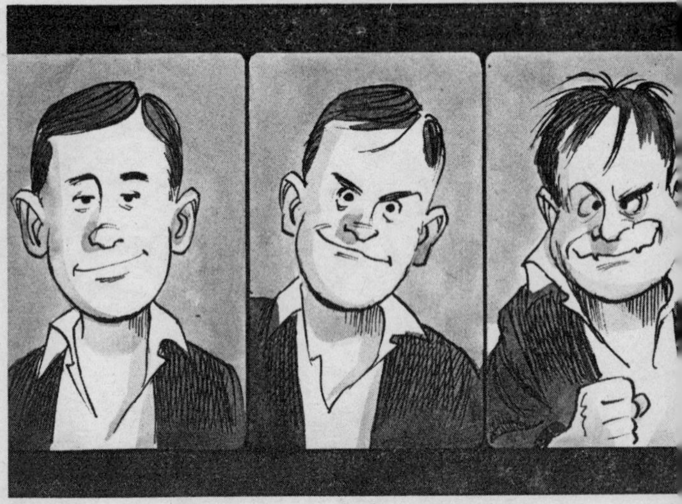

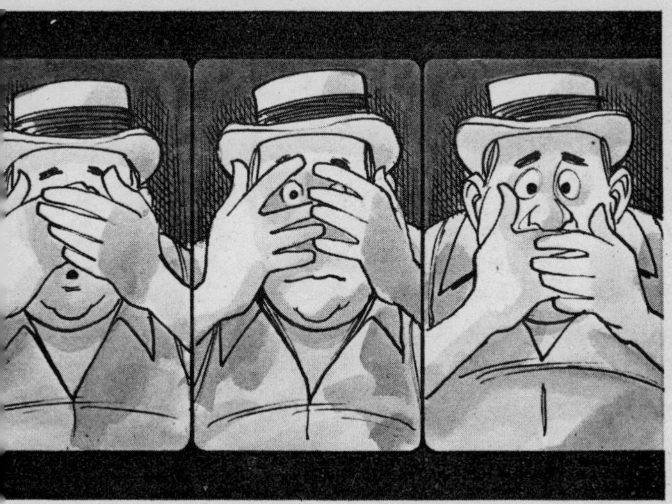

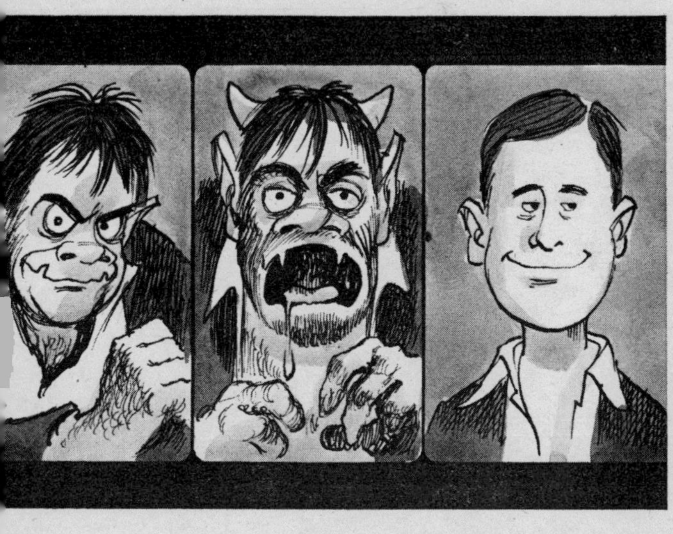

If The Mafia Were Run Like A Professional Sport

Mafia League Superstars

Danny "Horse" DeCarlo
Left Hood
New York Stranglers

During crucial contests with opposing mobs, DeCarlo waits on the sidelines to bring in the chains, usually to wrap around the neck of a rival hit-man. Lean, muscular and illiterate, DeCarlo has a high tolerance of pain, so long as it's being endured by a dying player of the opposition.

44

Vito Tuttifrutti
Right Gun
Detroit Crunchers

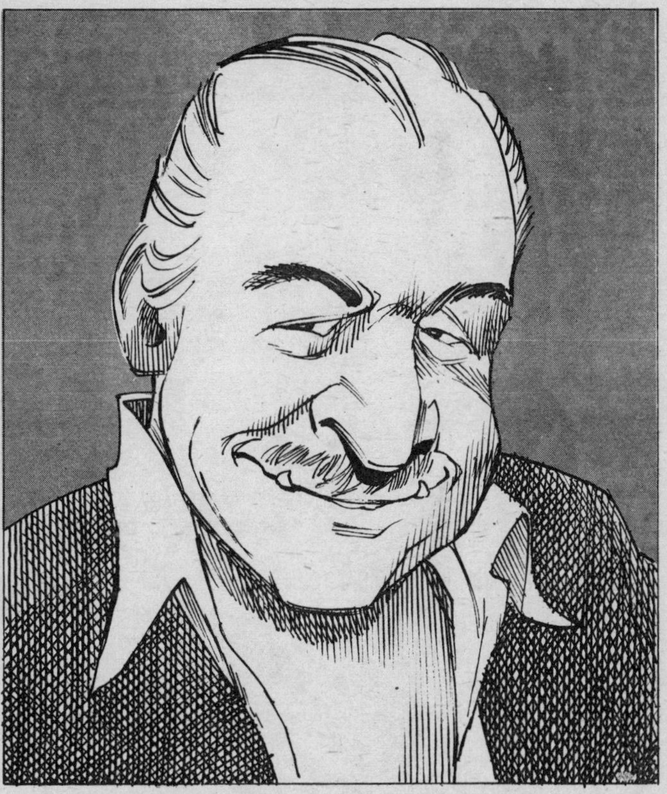

Tuttifrutti attracted notice in 1974 when, after Chicago refused to fold in the playoffs, he eliminated them singlehandedly with a shotgun. This feat earned him Rookie of the Year honors and the right to beat up anyone in Michigan whose last name begins with an "R." Popular with his teammates, Tuttifrutti spends his spare time pummeling blind newsdealers.

Cosmo Spinelli
Designated Crippler
Philadelphia Goons

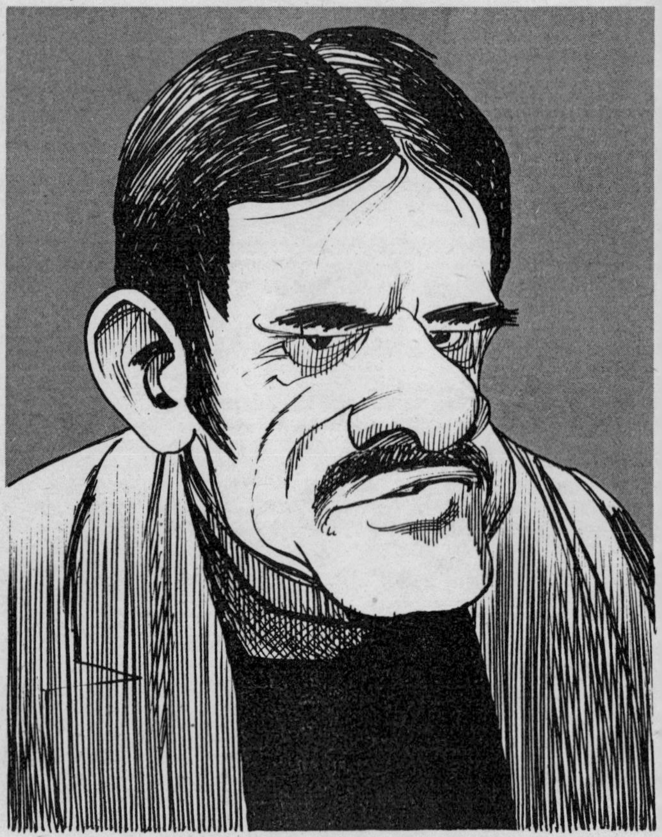

Spinelli was a part of the now-famous Philadelphia-Houston trade of 1969, in which he came to Philadelphia in return for squealer Peppe "Snake" Olivetti, who was sent to Houston in a casket. Spinelli has proved a "find," coming off the bench time and again to choke off opposing rallies with his bare hands.

Marco "Hulk" Marconi
Monsterman
Chicago Crushers

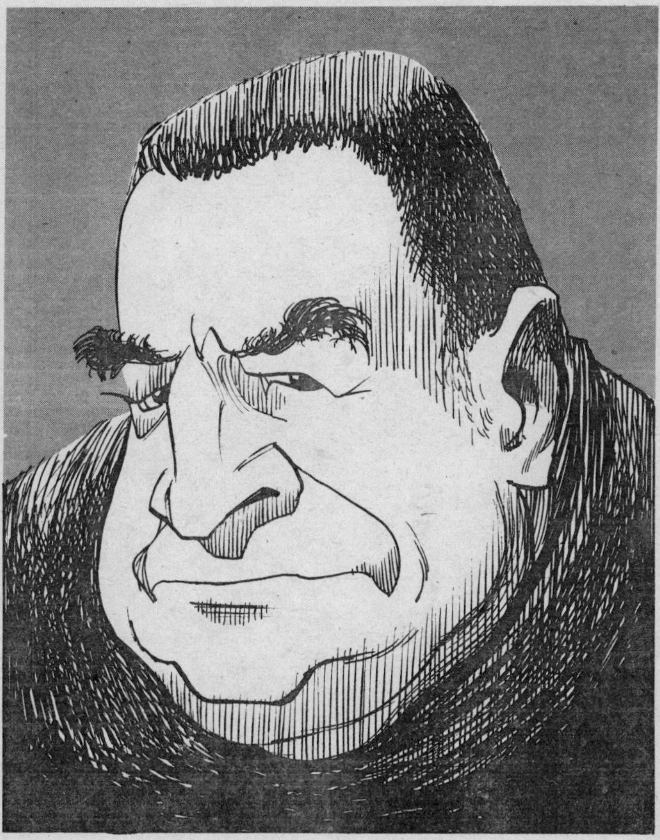

Marconi has carved out a name for himself, most recently on the forehead of Fats Orsini, the late 8th-round draft choice of the now-defunct Jersey City Gougers. Through 1976, Marconi ran the Chicago numbers racket until it was learned he couldn't count past 10. He stays in shape punching himself in the head.

Vincent "Ferret" Duomo
Offensive Creep
Houston Clouters

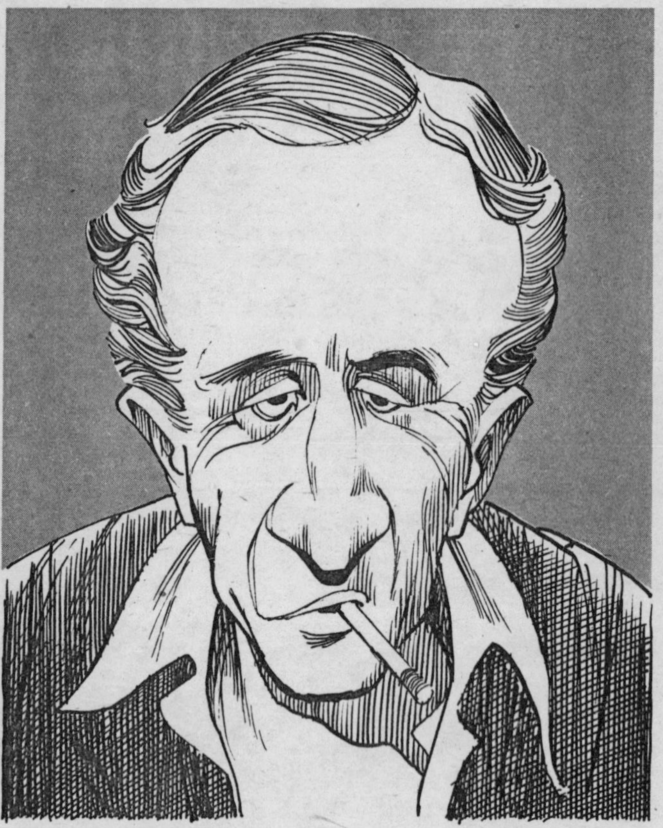

Duomo came to Houston after several seasons with the organization's farm-club in San Antonio, where he distinguished himself by selling protection to his parents. He's used mainly in "trap" plays, whereby he arranges peace parlays of rival mobs in restaurants, then plants explosive charges in the eggplant parmigian.

Salvatore "Floyd" Tartini
Team Captain and Maimer
St. Louis Stompers

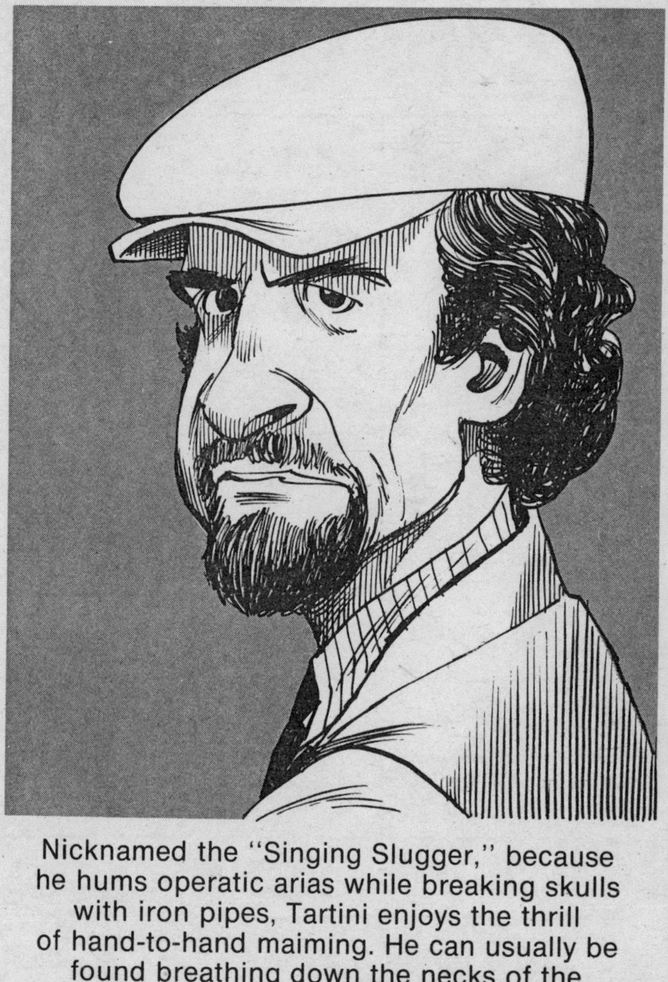

Nicknamed the "Singing Slugger," because he hums operatic arias while breaking skulls with iron pipes, Tartini enjoys the thrill of hand-to-hand maiming. He can usually be found breathing down the necks of the opposition, a maneuver made doubly effective because of his fondness for eating raw onions before a contest.

MAFIA
TEAM

CITY	Annual Take (Millions)[1]	Narcotics (millions)
New York	55.6	21.4
Chicago	49.5	18.6
Philadelphia	41.3	17.7
Los Angeles	38.8	20.2
Houston	35.4	11.5
St. Louis	29.2	10.7
Detroit	28.4	13.7
Boston	12.1[4]	2.9

1 Does not include birthday gifts, tributes ,etc.,
  received by Dons and Capos.
2 Trucks only. Does not include hijacking of cars,
  buses, bicycles or street pushcarts.

LEAGUE STANDINGS

Hijacks (millions)[2]	Loansharking (millions)	Profit Margin (%)
16.3	12.4	.642
21.4	7.5	.585
11.2	12.6	.542
9.8	7.6	.508
10.1	8.5	.486
13.2[3]	2.8	.456
11.2	3.2	.452
1.4	4.1	.288

3 Does not include 3 truckloads of Pampers mistaken for electrical appliances by "Shades" Barzini.
4 Season's opener delayed 9 weeks pending outcome of war between Salazzo and Petroni families.

Mafia League Meaning Of Lookout's Signals

INELIGIBLE RECEIVER

Our fence is an
undercover informer
for the Feds!

OFF-SIDE

We've just dumped him
off the side
of a pier!

OFFENSIVE INTERFERENCE

A rival Mob is
horning in on our
numbers racket!

OFFENSIVE HOLDING

They're holding
our Capo
hostage!

DEFENSIVE HOLDING

We're holding **their**
Capo hostage
in retaliation!

OFFSETTING PENALTIES

Both Capos
have been
bumped off!

FIRST & TEN

Our Hit-Man's been busted for the first time and been given 10 years!

PILING ON

The judge has added 15 years because of previous offenses!

ILLEGAL MOTION

Our attorney is bribing the judge to get the charge reduced to jaywalking!

TIME OUT

Our Hit-Man won't have to serve time and is being let out!

ILLEGAL PROCEDURE

That 5-pound bag of cocaine is filled with powdered sugar!

TWO-MINUTE WARNING

Our "Connection" has two minutes to get us "the good stuff" —or else!

ILLEGAL SHIFT

Our "Connection" is dealing with a rival mob!

RESUME PLAY

We've knocked off both the "Connection" **and** the rival mob!

MAFIA LEAGUE

PLAYER	Contracts	Hits
Fazool, Chi.	46	38
Linguini, N.Y.[1]	51	40
Spinelli, Phila.[2]	35	2?
Labonza, Boston	109	6?
Carbona, Detroit	76	4?
DeCarlo, N.Y.	77	3?
Zucchini, Houston	88	4
Tartini, St. Louis	67	29

1 Disappeared in middle of season.
2 Rubbed out in middle of season.
3 Includes taking 2 bum raps for Izzy "The Eel" Ronzon?

LEADERS

Double-Crosses	Busts	Slugging Average
12	5	.826
14	6	.784
8	3	.771
19	11[3]	.606
10	5	.579
9	2	.506[4]
2	9	.466
11	7	.432

4 Average may be increased if body brought up from East River proves to be "Big Louie" Ferrara.
5 Does not include August 8 massacre at Charlie's Bar & Grill.

A TV Interview with a Mafia League Coach

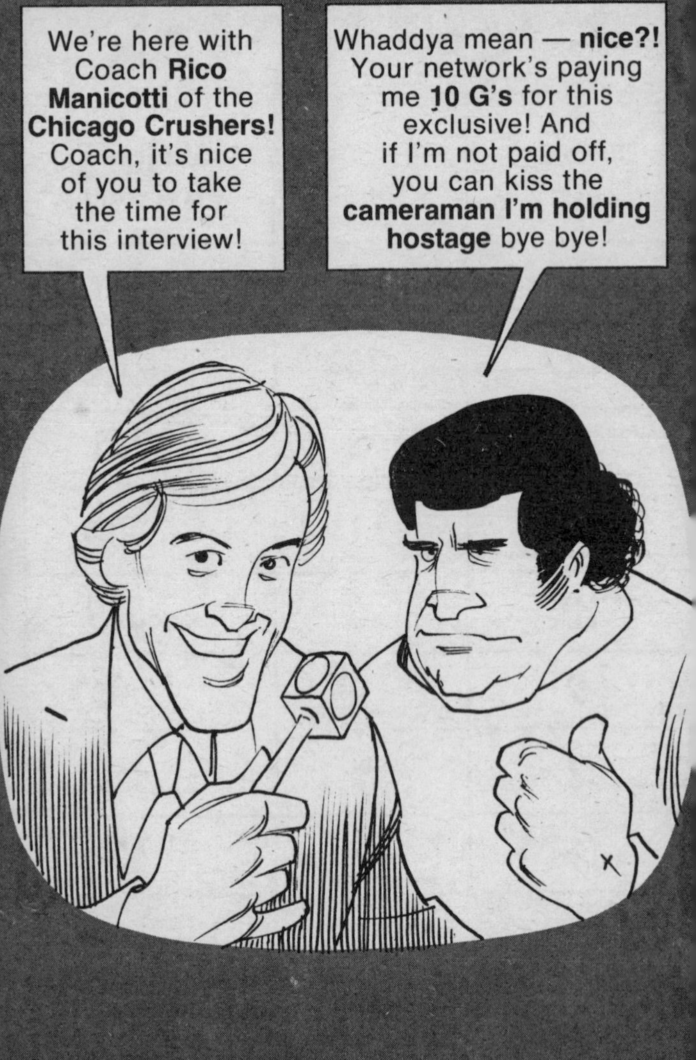

We're here with Coach **Rico Manicotti** of the **Chicago Crushers!** Coach, it's nice of you to take the time for this interview!
Whaddya mean — **nice?!** Your network's paying me **10 G's** for this exclusive! And if I'm not paid off, you can kiss the **cameraman I'm holding hostage** bye bye!

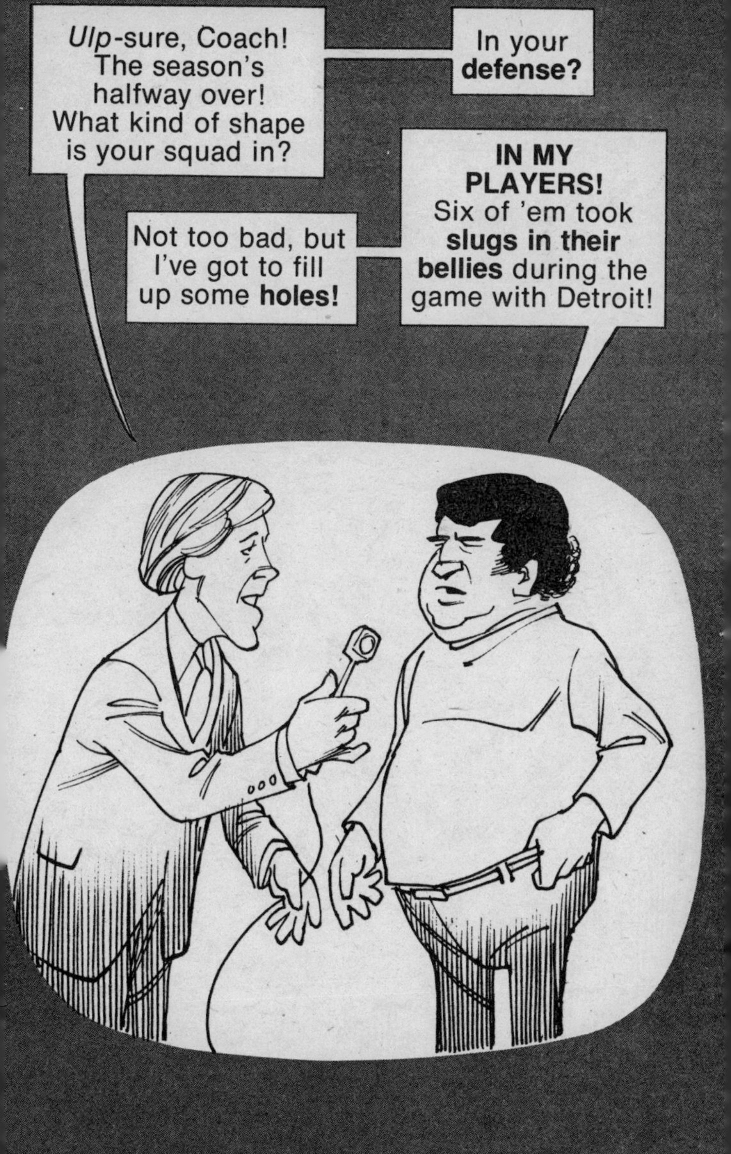

Ulp-sure, Coach! The season's halfway over! What kind of shape is your squad in?
Not too bad, but I've got to fill up some **holes!**
In your **defense?**
IN MY PLAYERS! Six of 'em took **slugs in their bellies** during the game with Detroit!

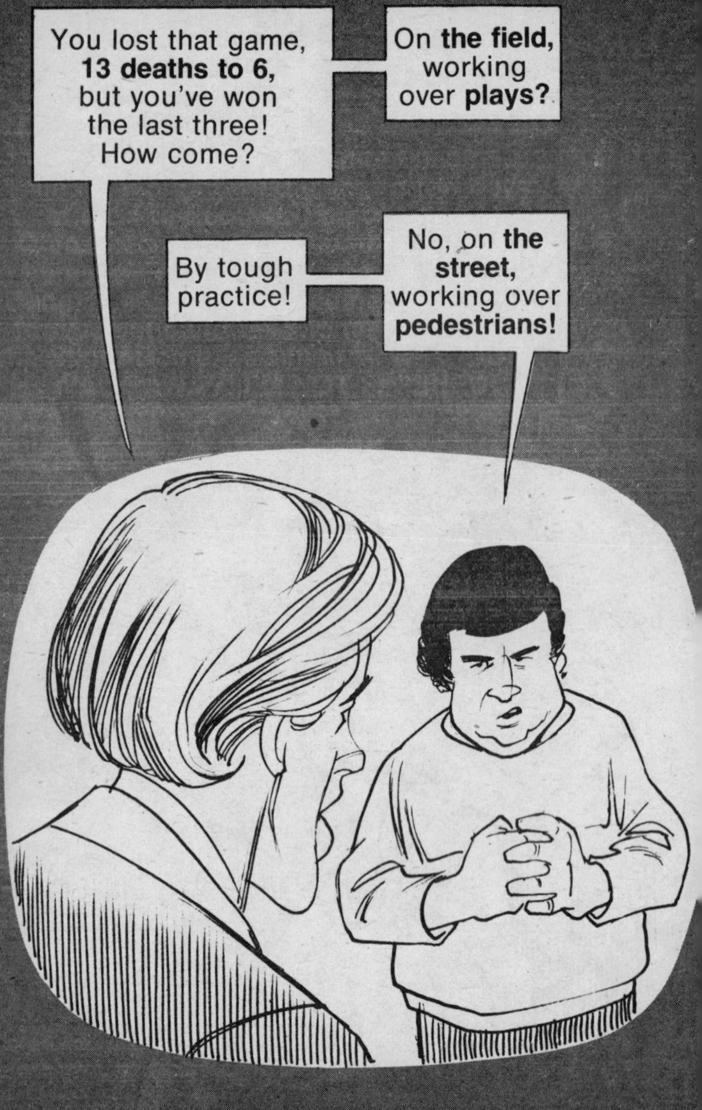

You lost that game, 13 deaths to 6, but you've won the last three! How come?
On the field, working over plays?
By tough practice!
No, on the street, working over pedestrians!

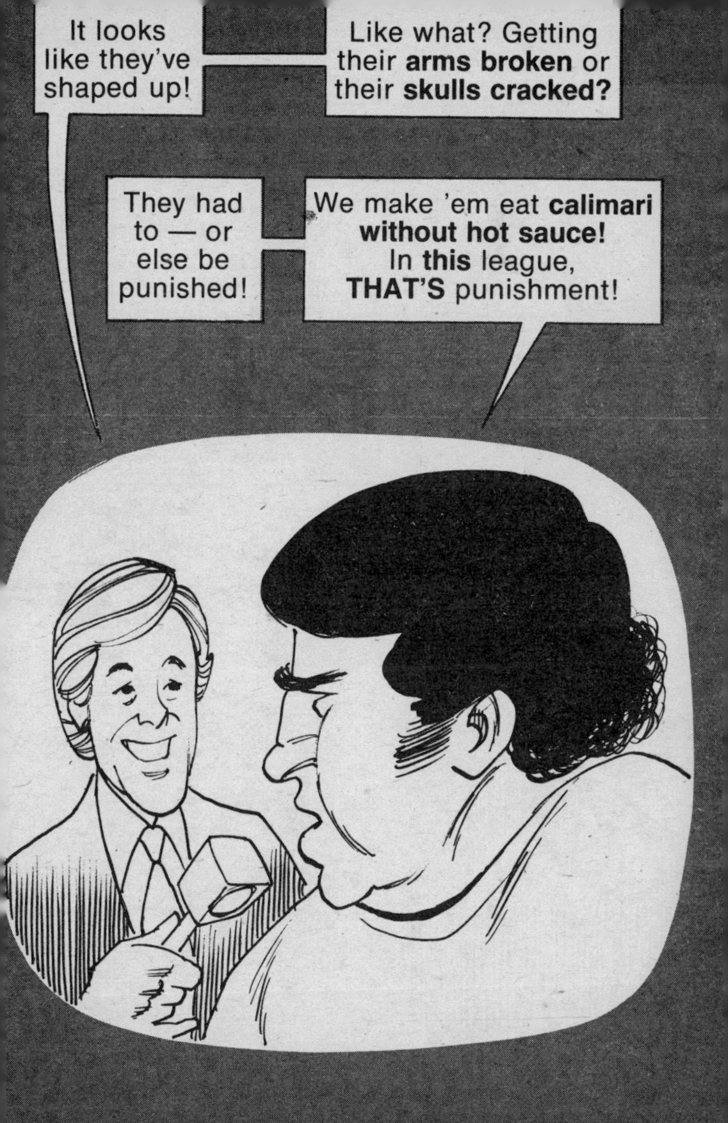
It looks like they've shaped up!
Like what? Getting their **arms broken** or their **skulls cracked?**
They had to — or else be punished!
We make 'em eat **calimari without hot sauce!** In **this** league, **THAT'S** punishment!

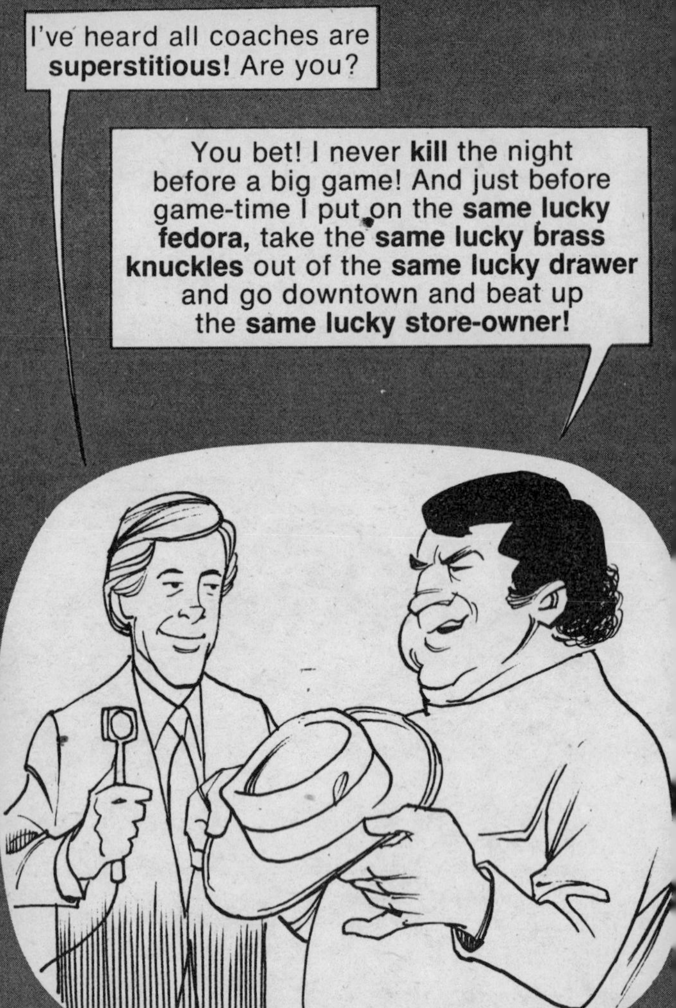
I've heard all coaches are **superstitious!** Are you?
You bet! I never **kill** the night before a big game! And just before game-time I put on the **same lucky fedora,** take the **same lucky brass knuckles** out of the **same lucky drawer** and go downtown and beat up the **same lucky store-owner!**

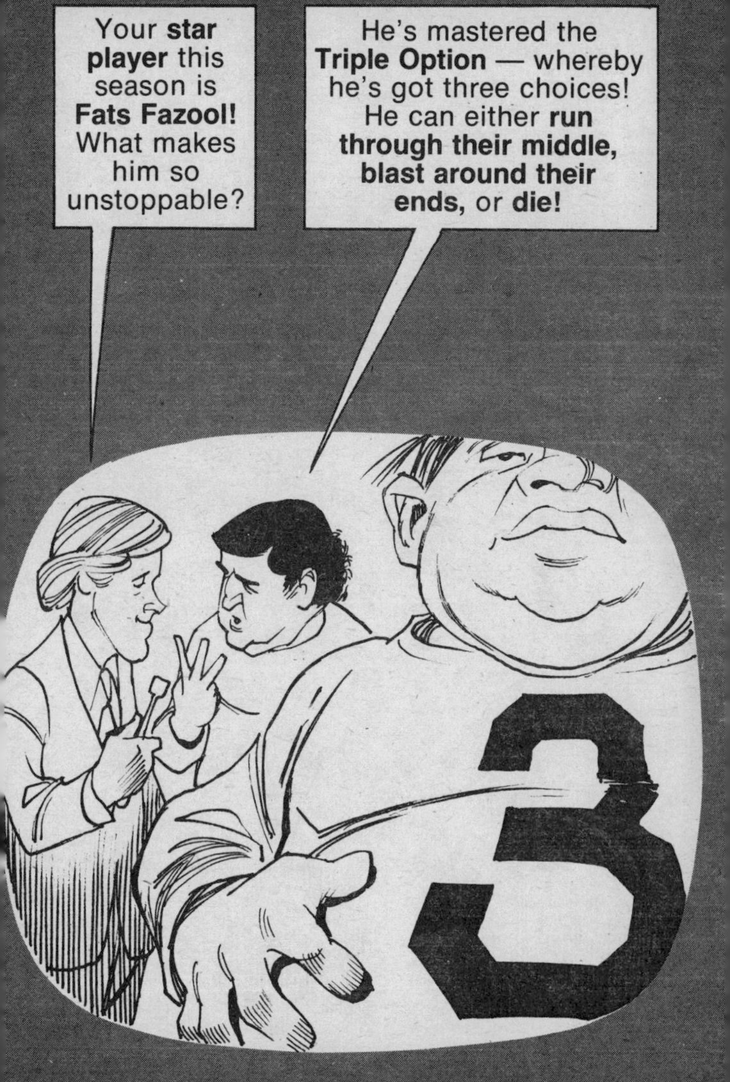
Your **star player** this season is **Fats Fazool!** What makes him so unstoppable?
He's mastered the **Triple Option** — whereby he's got three choices! He can either **run through their middle, blast around their ends,** or **die!**
3

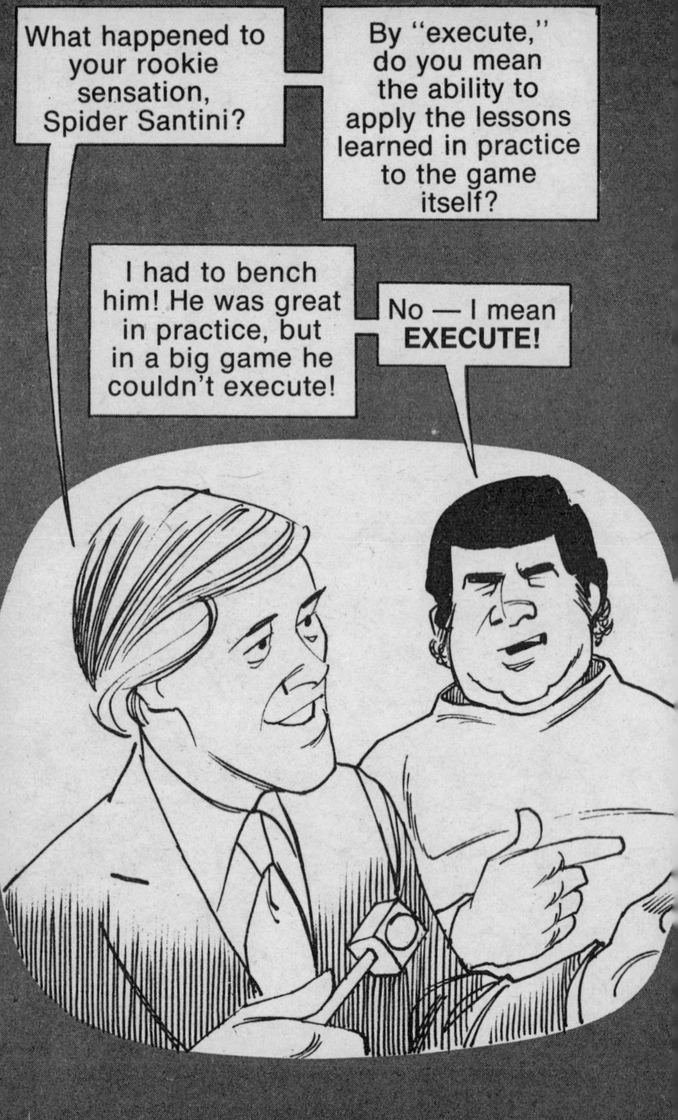
What happened to your rookie sensation, Spider Santini?
By "execute," do you mean the ability to apply the lessons learned in practice to the game itself?
I had to bench him! He was great in practice, but in a big game he couldn't execute!
No — I mean **EXECUTE!**

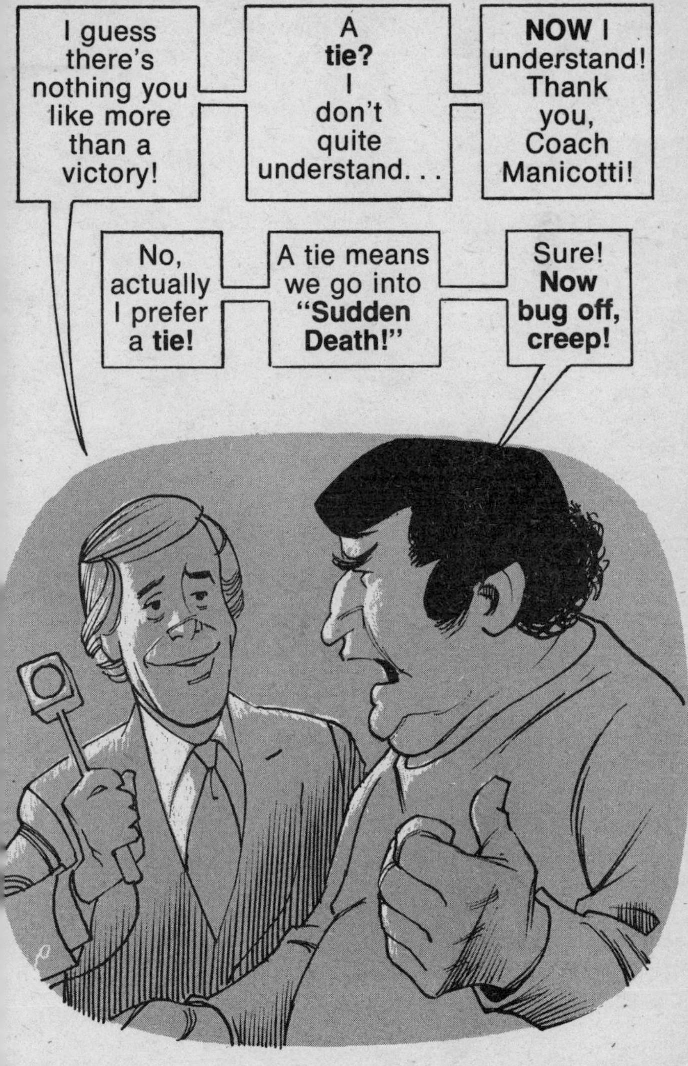
I guess there's nothing you like more than a victory!
A **tie?** I don't quite understand. . .
NOW I understand! Thank you, Coach Manicotti!
No, actually I prefer a **tie!**
A tie means we go into "**Sudden Death!**"
Sure! **Now bug off, creep!**

The Sports Lovers'
HATE BOOK

Don't you hate . . .

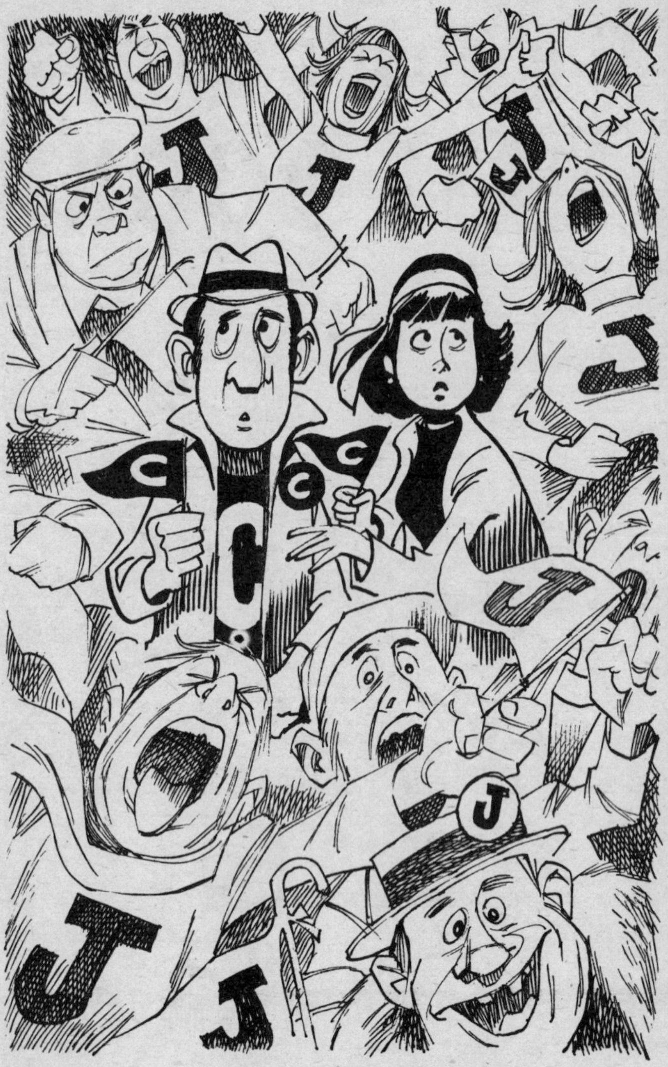

. . . paying $50 for two seats and finding they're in the opposing team's rooting section?

Don't you hate . . .

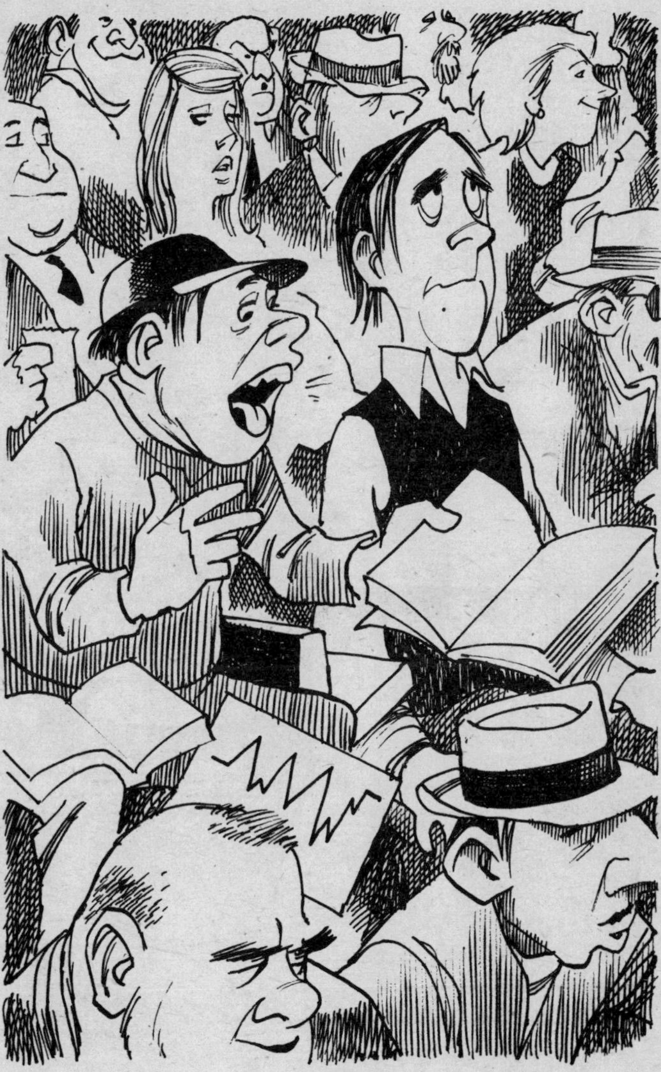

. . . sitting next to an "expert" who bores you with meaningless statistics between every pitch?

Don't you hate . . .

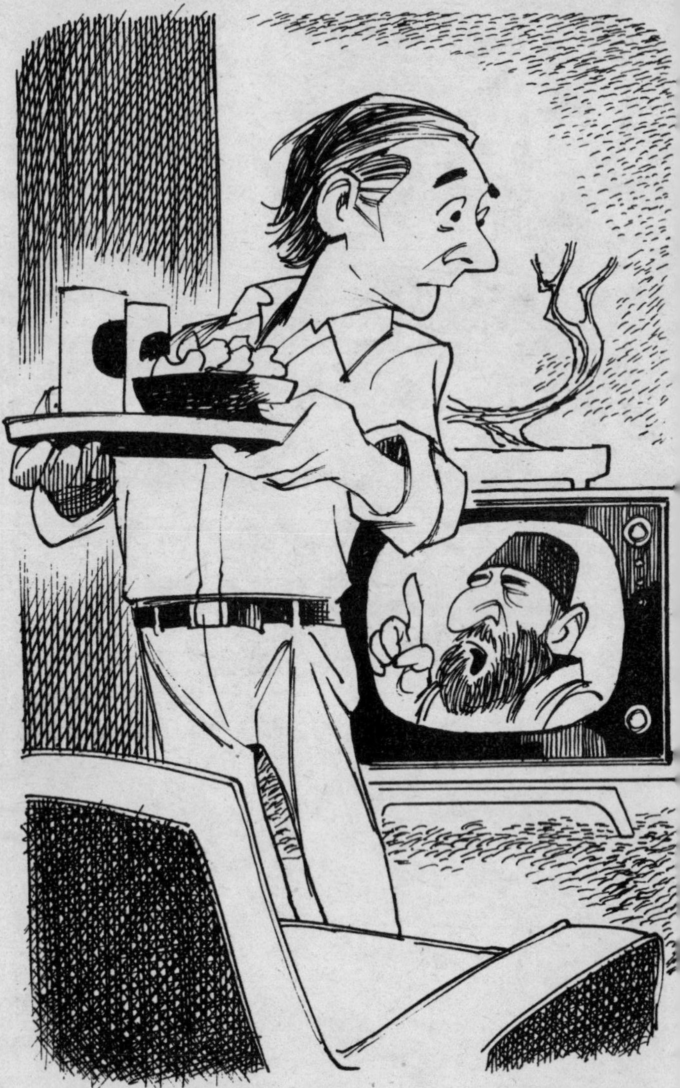

. . . when the Game of the Year is pre-empted by a United Nations Security Council meeting?

Don't you hate . . .

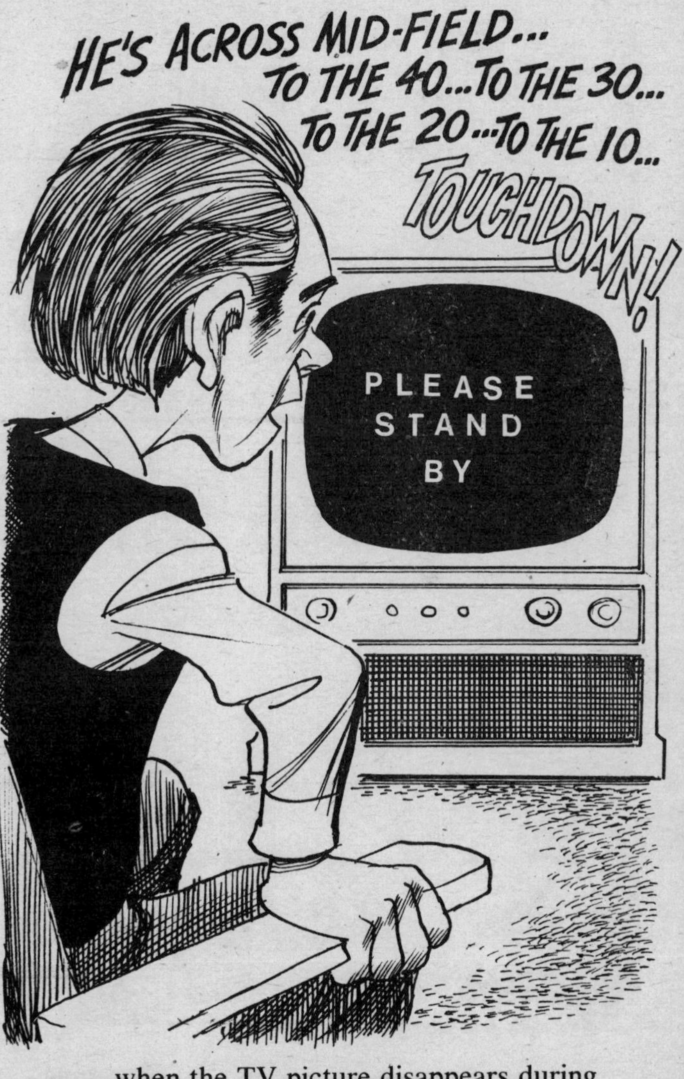
HE'S ACROSS MID-FIELD...
TO THE 40...TO THE 30...
TO THE 20...TO THE 10...
TOUCHDOWN!
PLEASE STAND BY

. . . when the TV picture disappears during the most crucial play of the game?

Don't you hate . . .

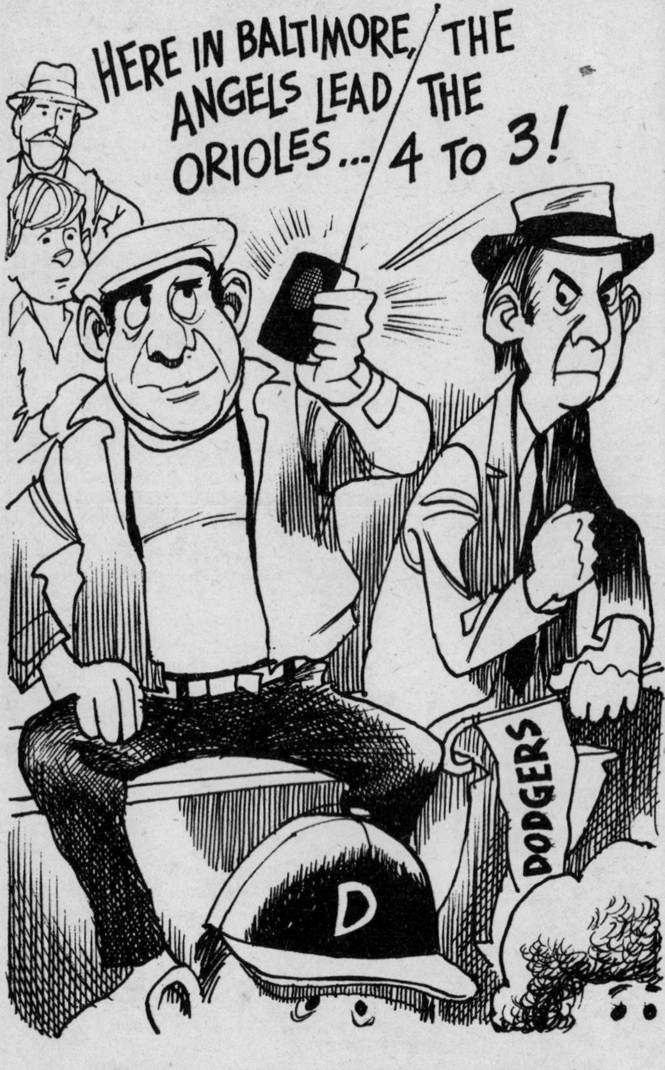

HERE IN BALTIMORE, THE ANGELS LEAD THE ORIOLES... 4 TO 3!
DODGERS
D

. . . sitting next to some idiot who's listening to another game on his transistor?

Don't you hate . . .

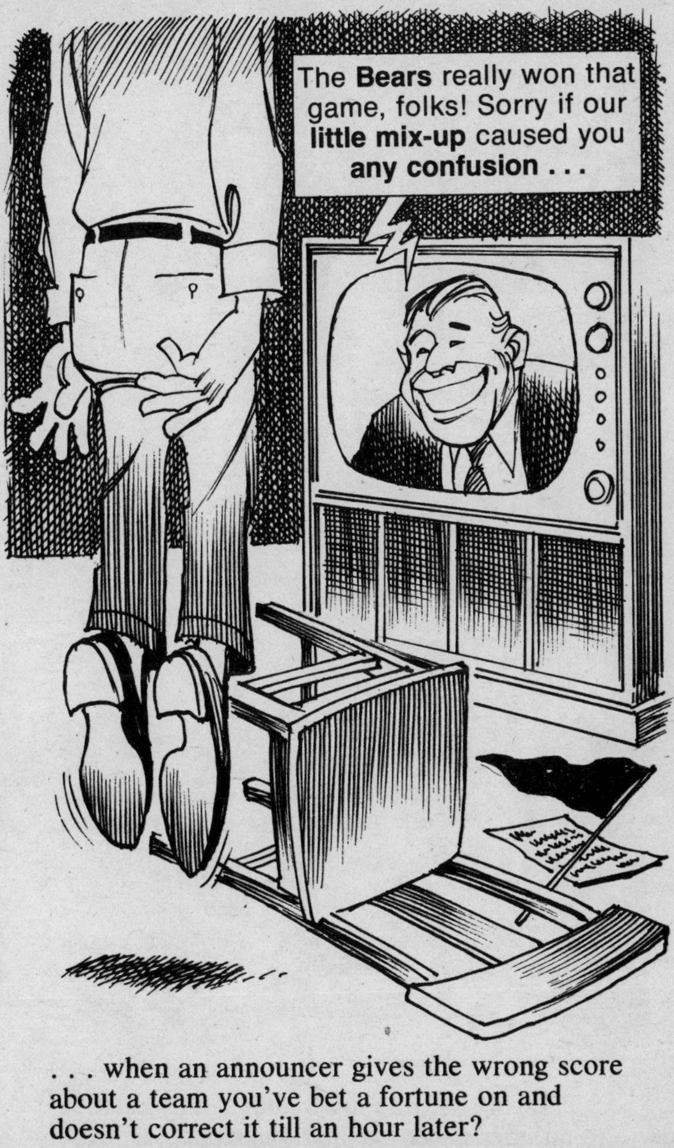
The **Bears** really won that game, folks! Sorry if our **little mix-up** caused you **any confusion . . .**

. . . when an announcer gives the wrong score about a team you've bet a fortune on and doesn't correct it till an hour later?

Don't you hate . . .

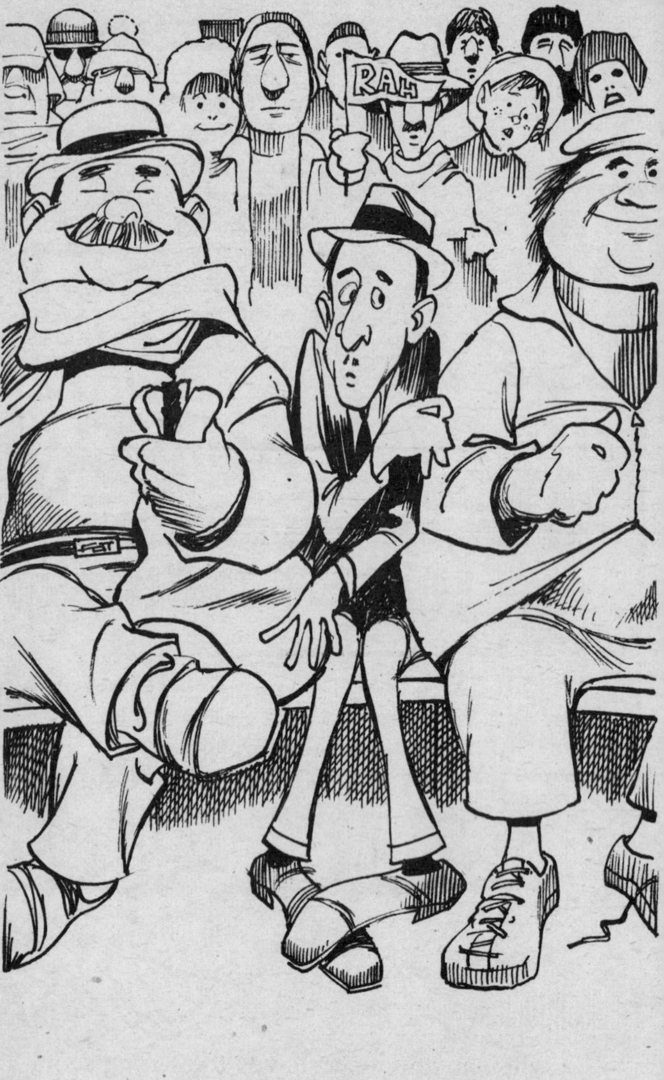

RAH

...buying a season ticket and finding you're sitting between two 300 pound people?

Don't you hate . . .

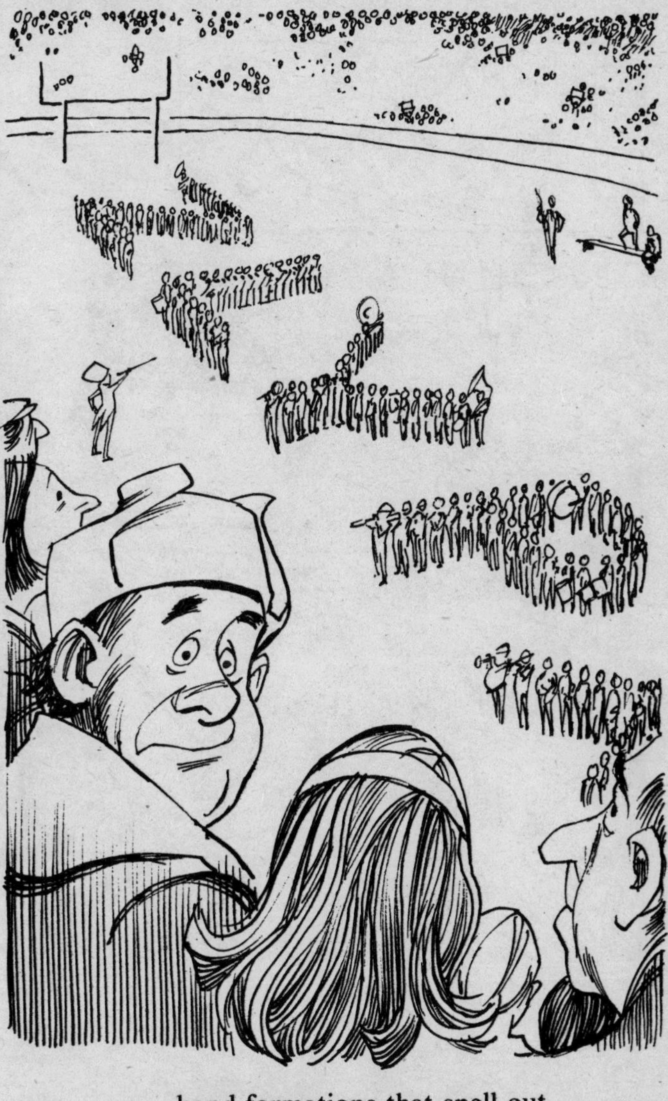

. . . band formations that spell out words you don't understand?

Don't you hate . . .

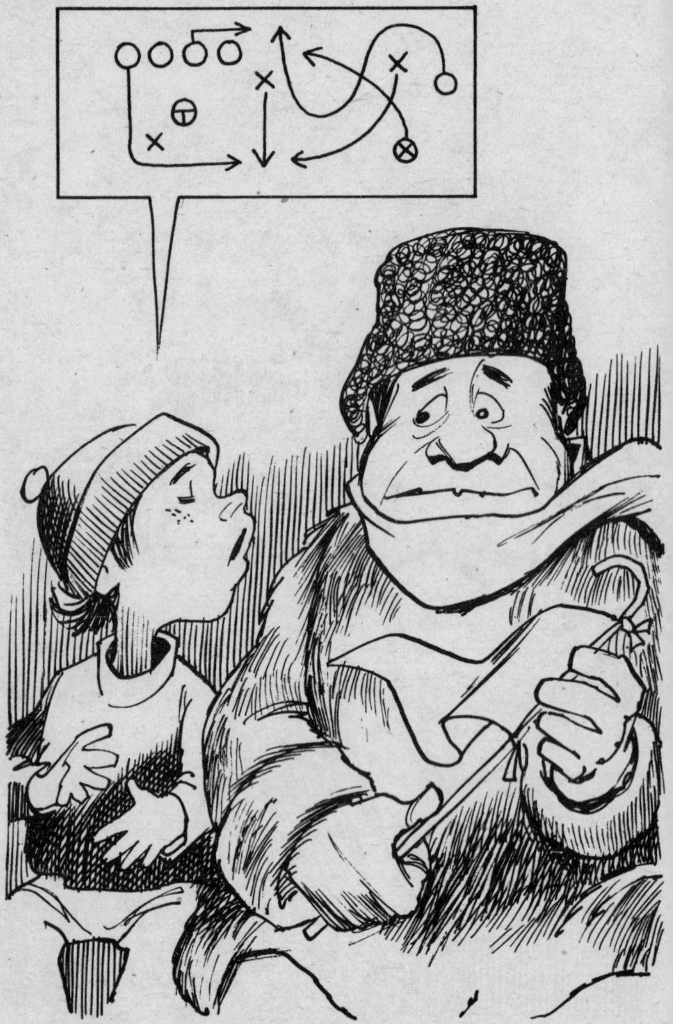

. . . sitting next to someone who knows more about the game than you do?

Don't you hate . . .

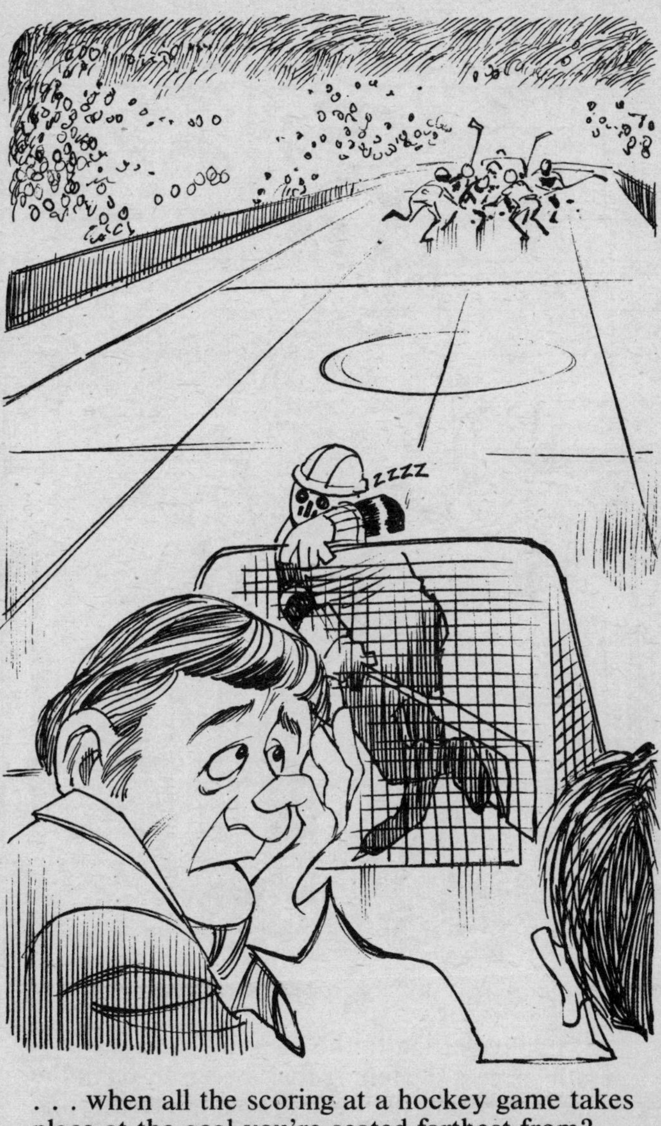

ZZZZ

. . . when all the scoring at a hockey game takes place at the goal you're seated farthest from?

Don't you hate . . .

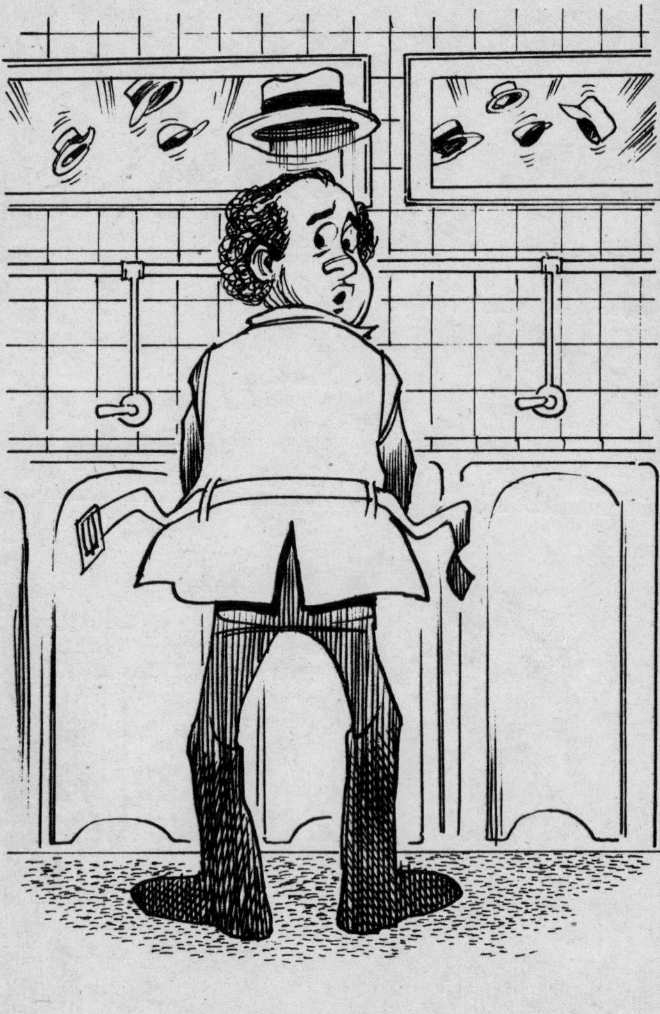

. . . finally getting to the john between halves and hearing a deafening roar sweep through the stands, meaning the Second Half is starting and something incredible is happening on the field?

Don't you hate . . .

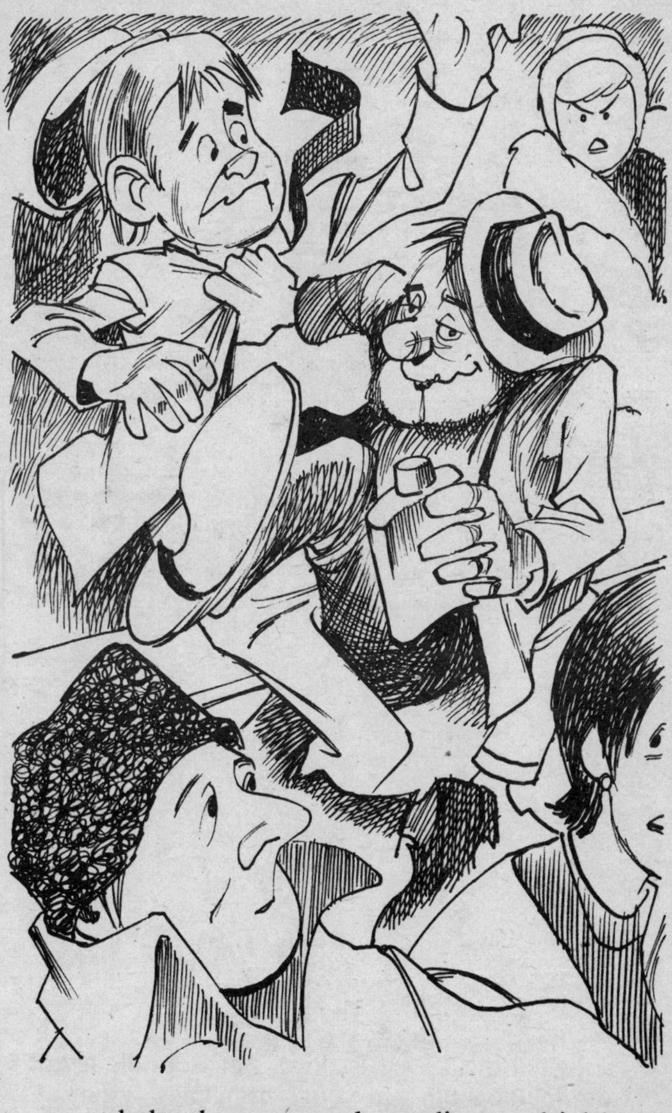

. . . clods who come to the stadium to drink?

Don't you hate . . .

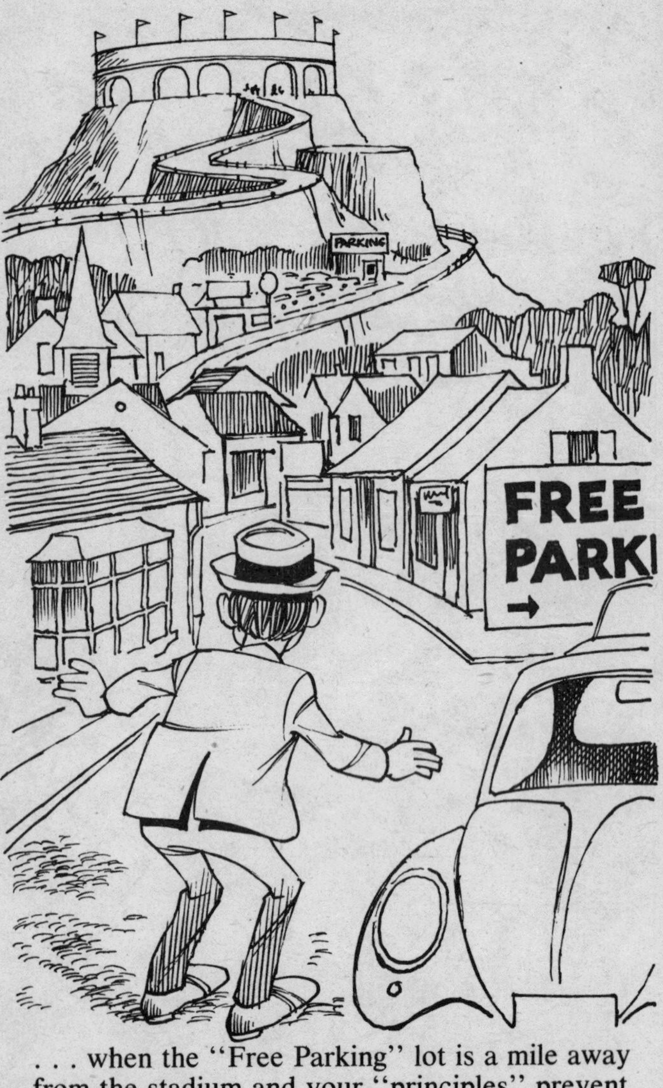
PARKING
FREE
PARK
→

. . . when the "Free Parking" lot is a mile away from the stadium and your "principles" prevent your paying $4.50 to park in a closer private lot?

Don't you hate . . .

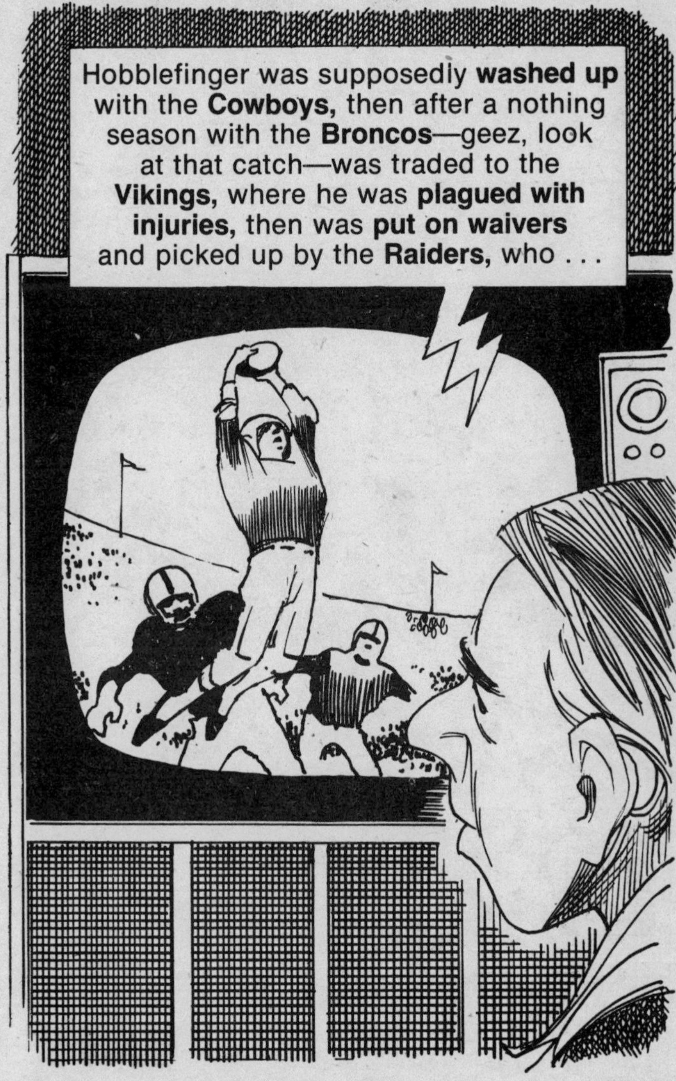
Hobblefinger was supposedly **washed up** with the **Cowboys,** then after a nothing season with the **Broncos**—geez, look at that catch—was traded to the **Vikings,** where he was **plagued with injuries,** then was **put on waivers** and picked up by the **Raiders,** who . . .

. . . sports announcers who talk too much?

Don't you hate . . .

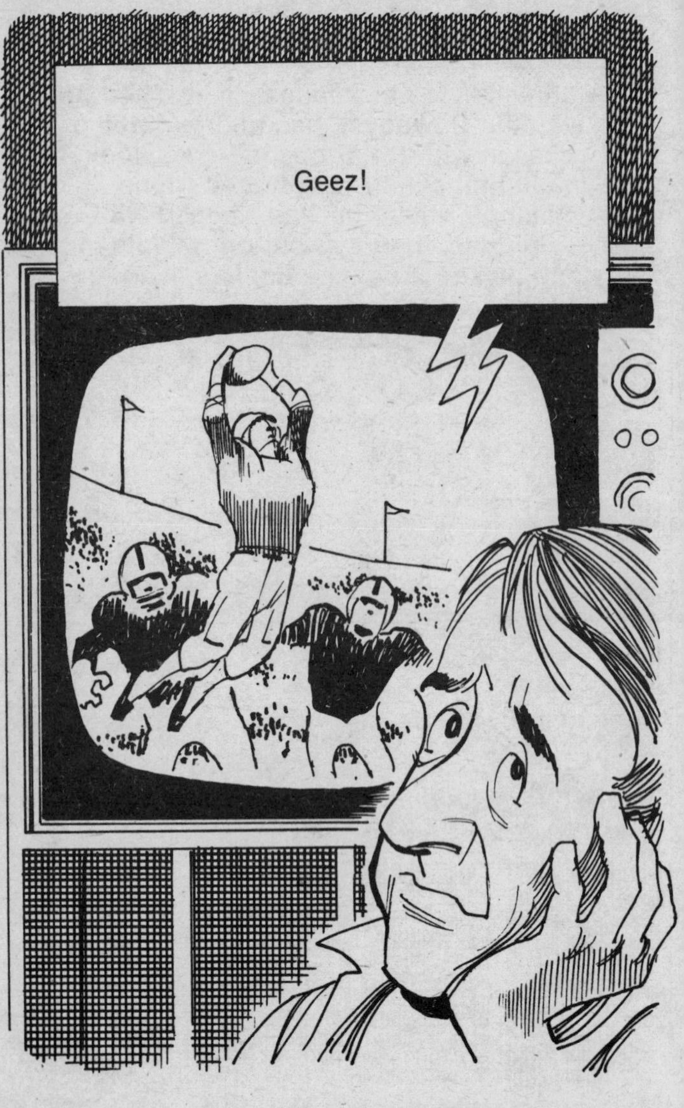
Geez!

. . . sports announcers who talk too little?

Don't you hate . . .

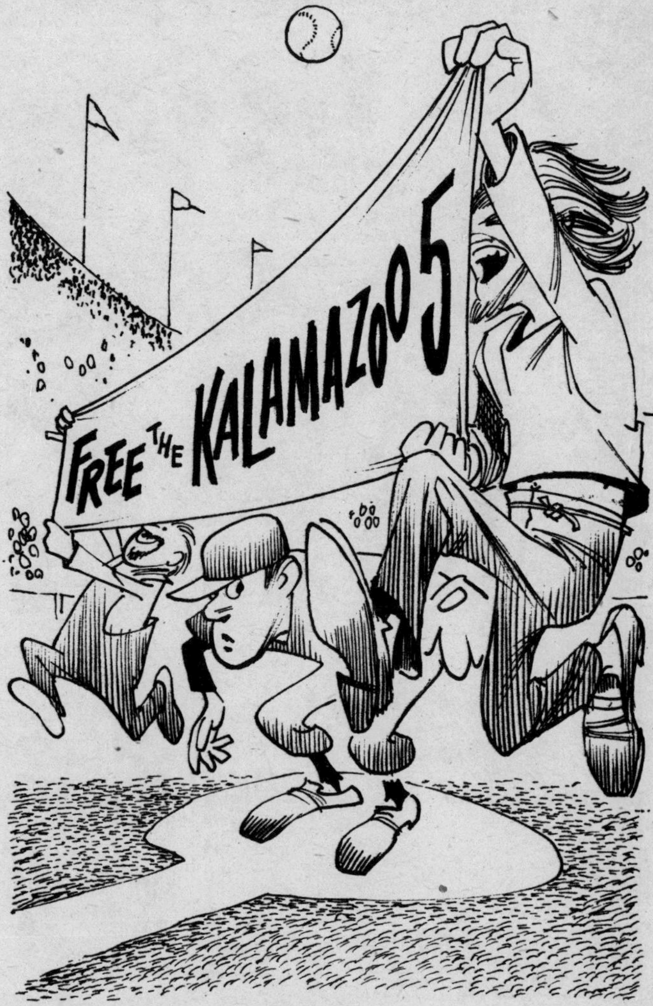
FREE THE KALAMAZOO 5

. . . nuts who run onto the playing field to draw attention to some idiot cause?

Don't you hate . . .

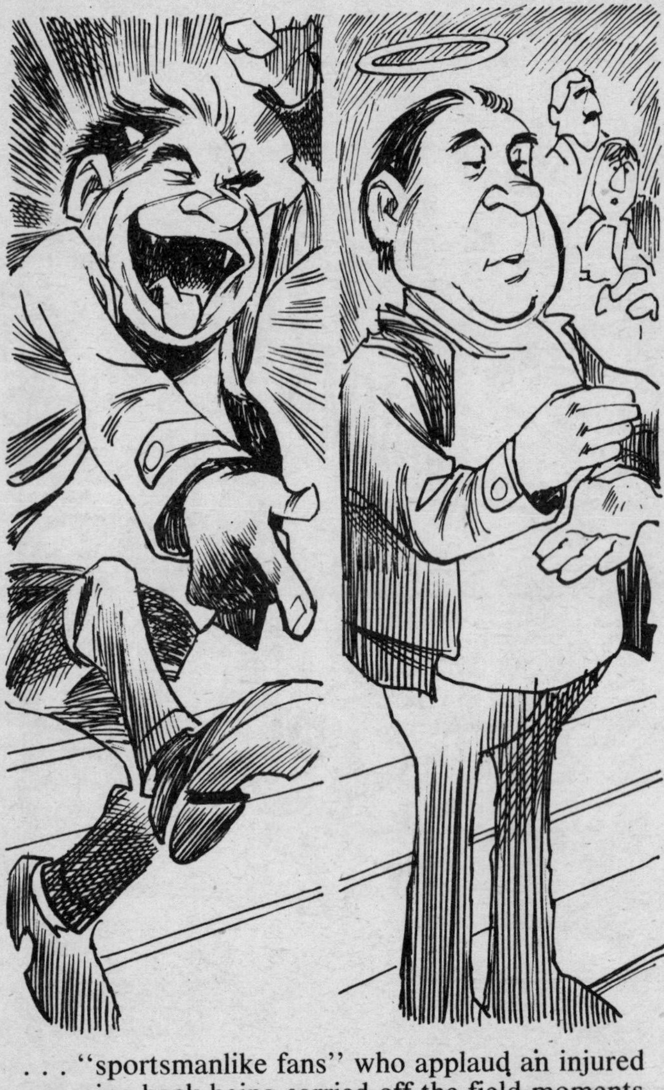

. . . "sportsmanlike fans" who applaud an injured opposing back being carried off the field moments after screaming with joy when he was creamed?

Don't you hate . . .

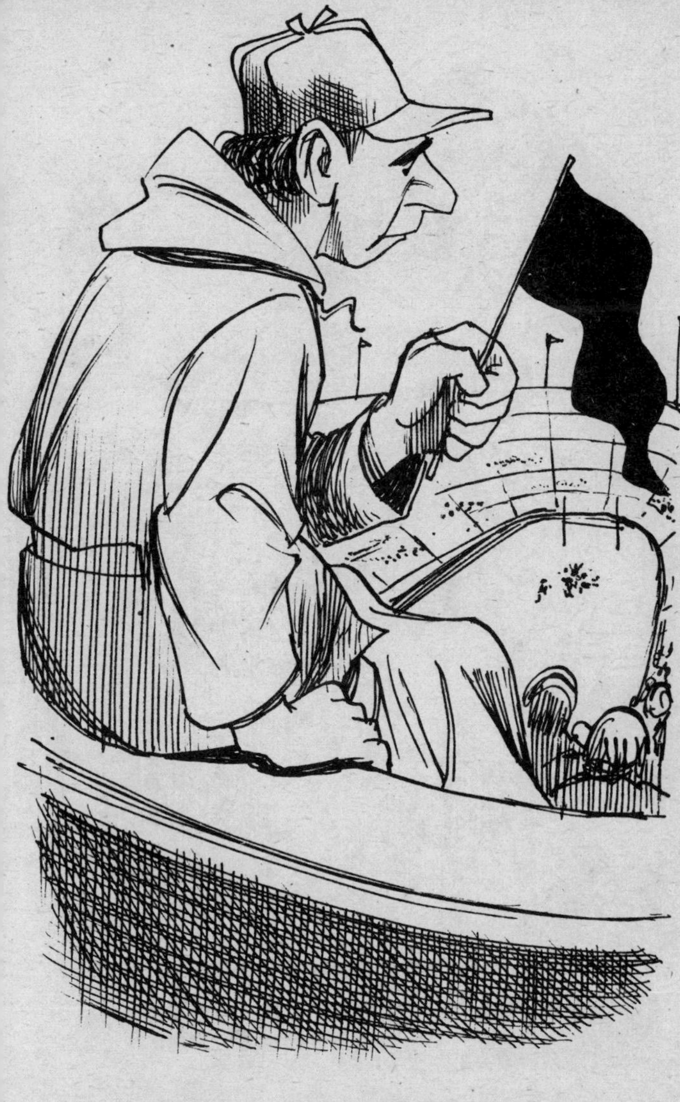

. . . watching a game from the top row of one of the new, mammoth Superdomes?

Don't you hate . . .

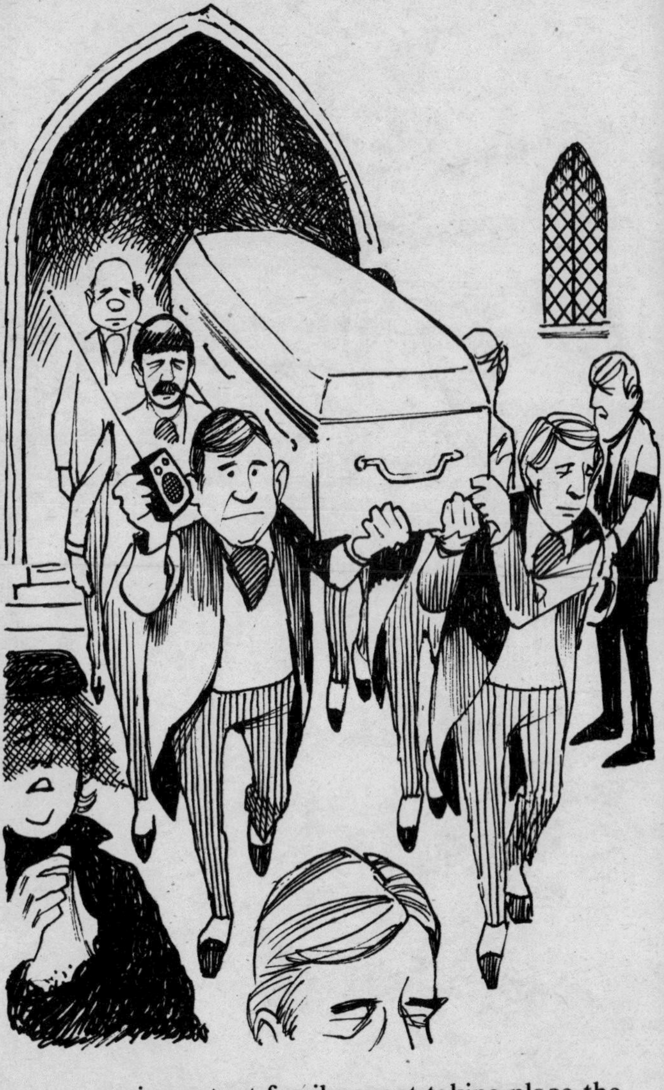

. . . an important family event taking place the day of the game you've waited all year to see?

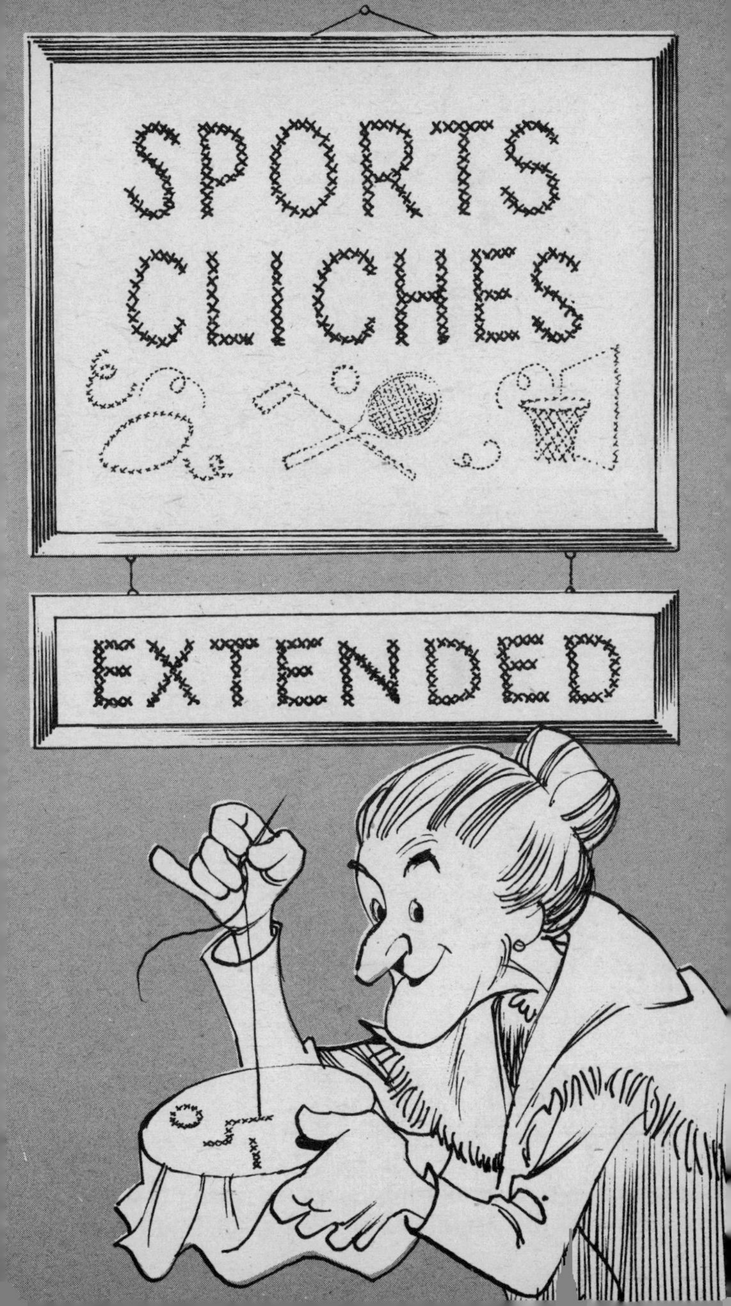
SPORTS CLICHES
EXTENDED

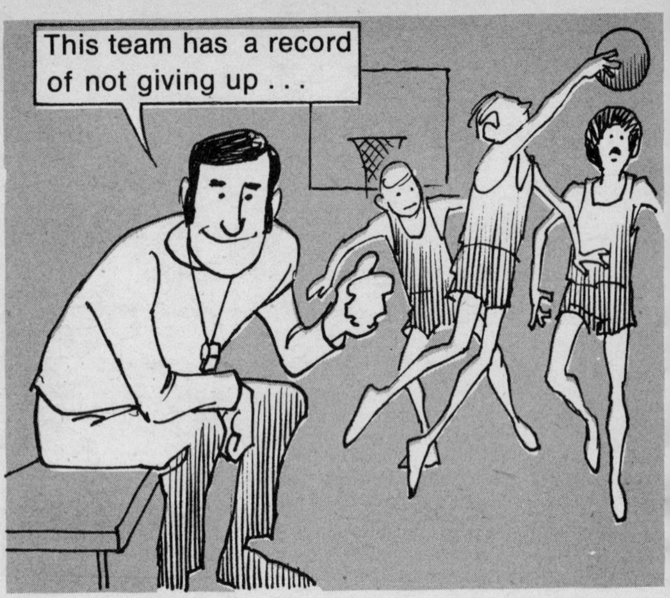
This team has a record of not giving up . . .

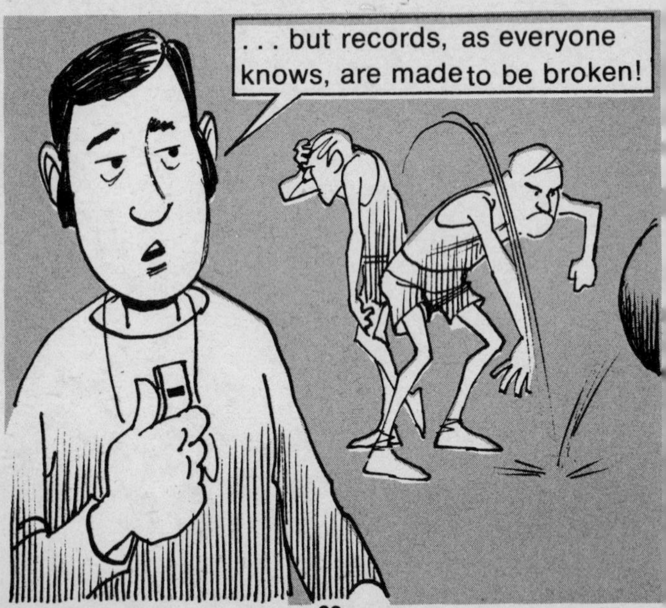
. . . but records, as everyone knows, are made to be broken!

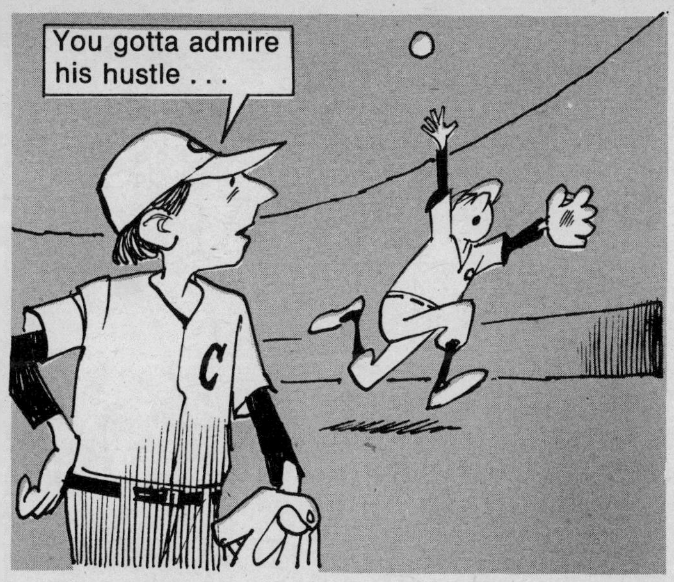
You gotta admire his hustle . . .

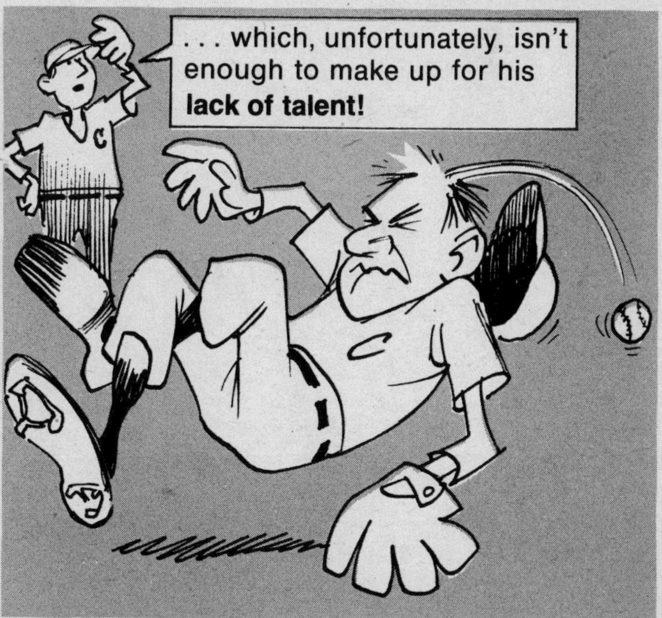
. . . which, unfortunately, isn't enough to make up for his **lack of talent!**

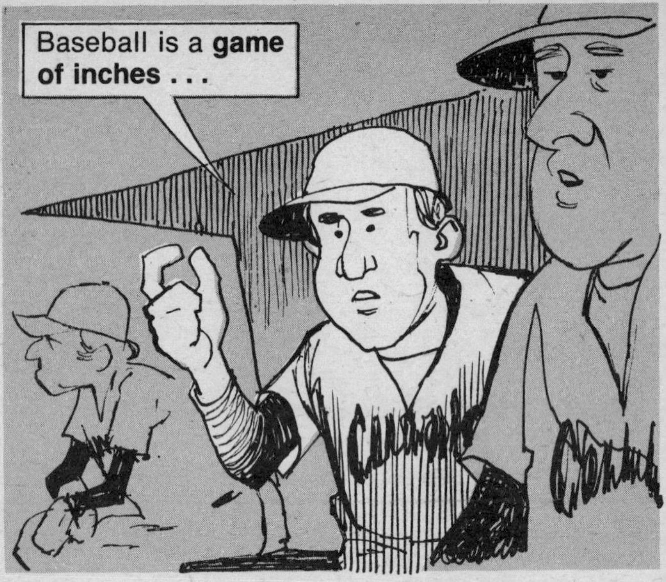
Baseball is a **game of inches . . .**

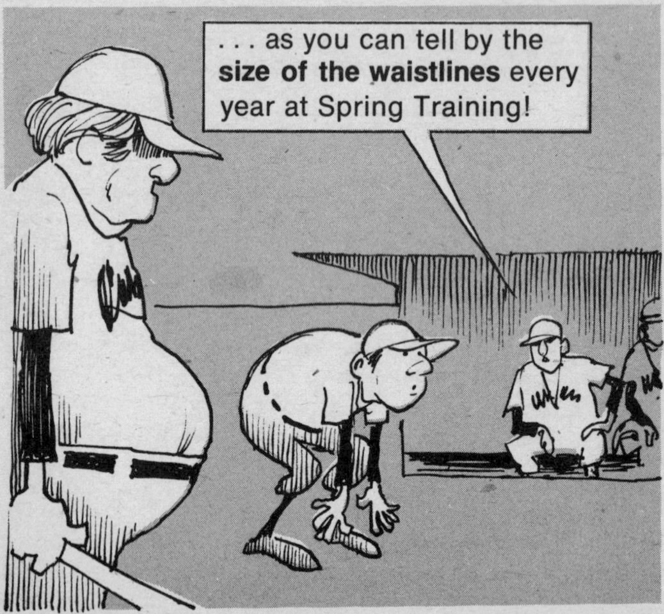
. . . as you can tell by the **size of the waistlines** every year at Spring Training!

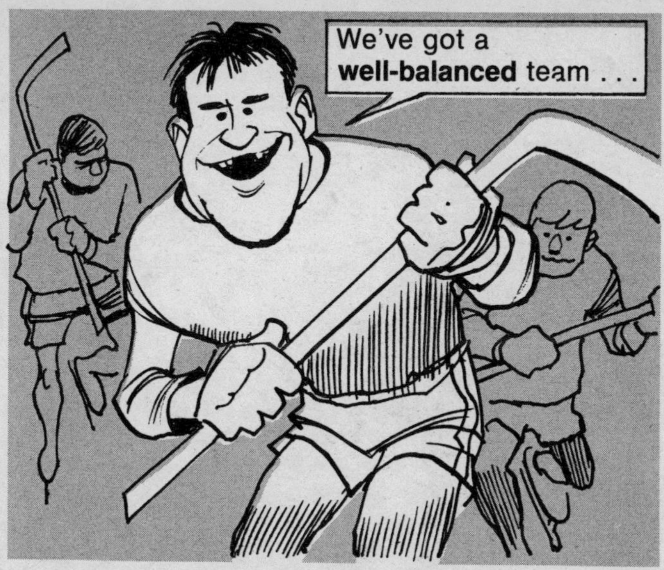
We've got a **well-balanced** team . . .

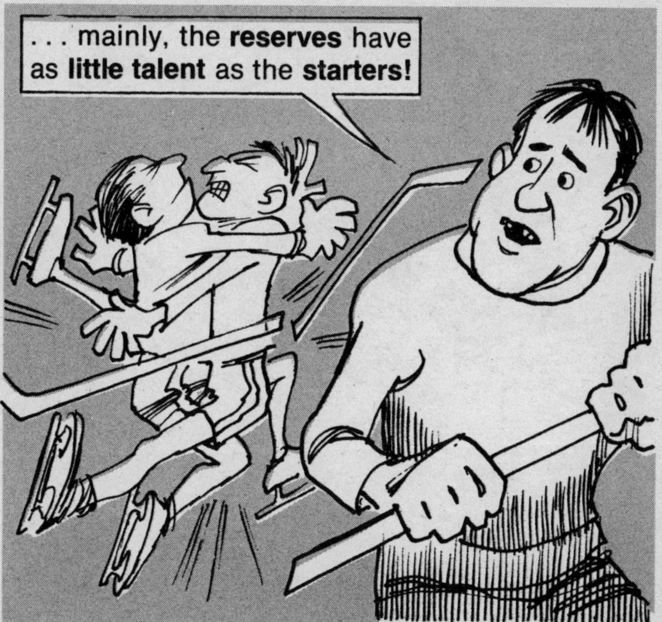
. . . mainly, the **reserves** have as **little talent** as the **starters!**

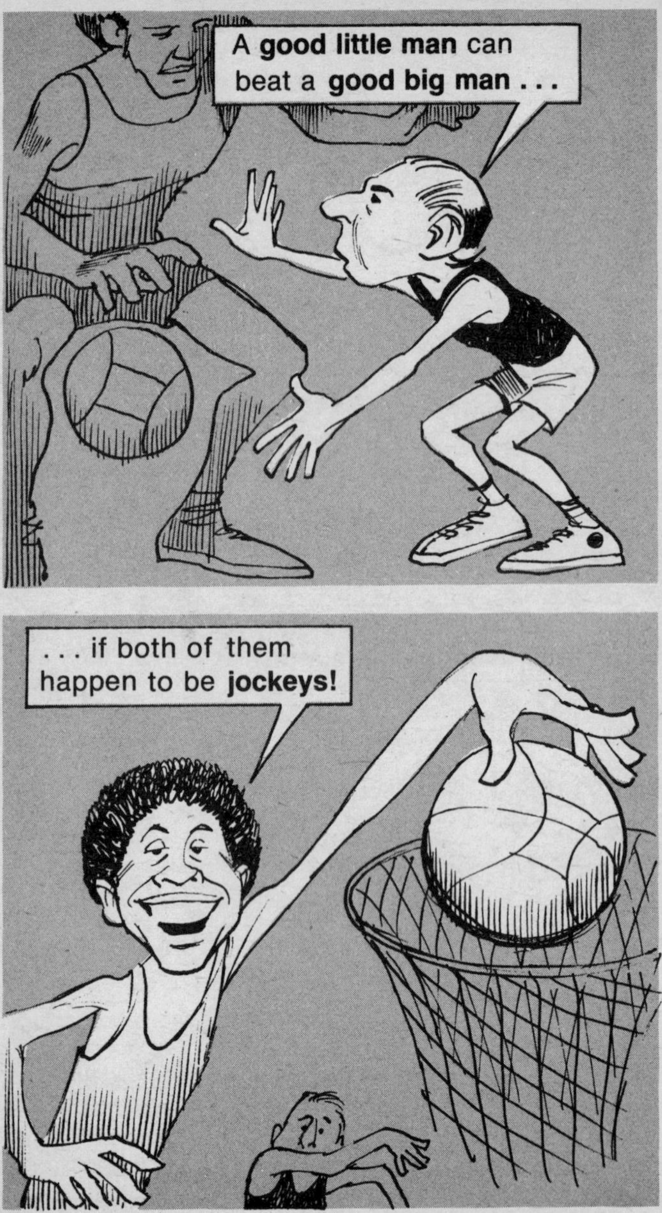
A **good little man** can beat a **good big man** . . .
. . . if both of them happen to be **jockeys**!

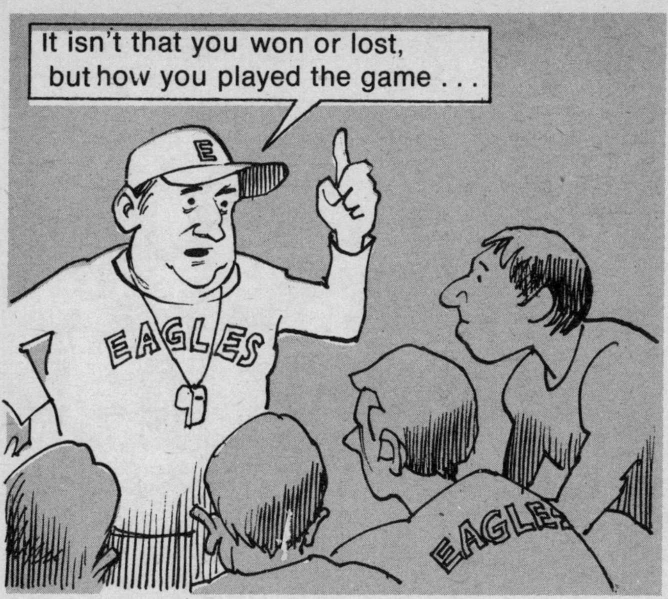
It isn't that you won or lost, but how you played the game . . .
EAGLES
E
EAGLES

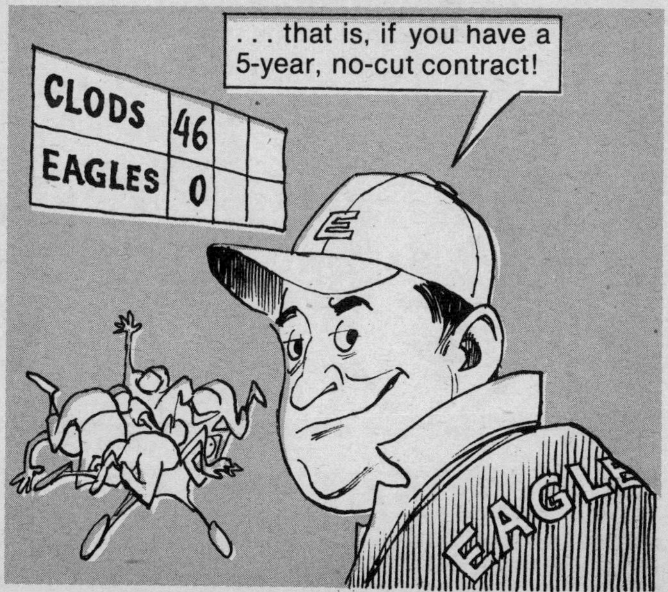
. . . that is, if you have a 5-year, no-cut contract!
CLODS 46
EAGLES 0
E

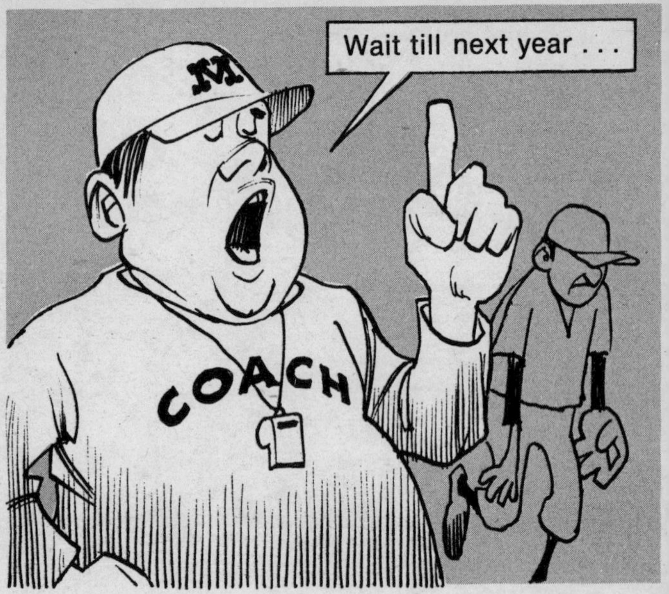
Wait till next year . . .
COACH

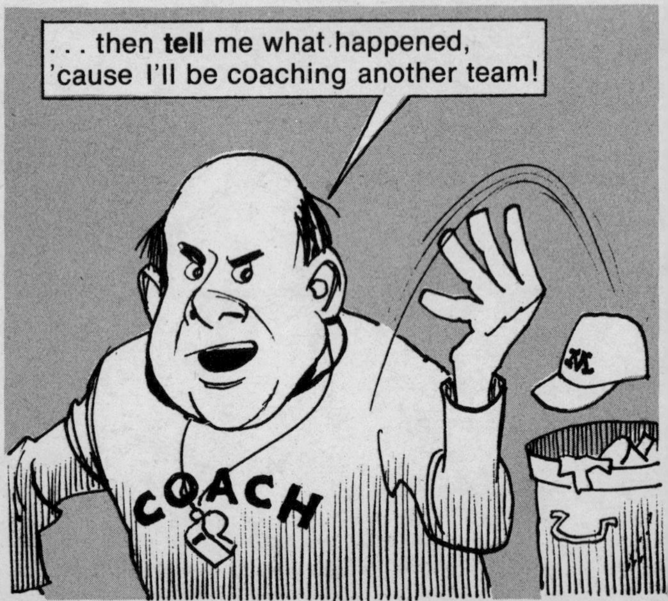
. . . then **tell** me what happened,
'cause I'll be coaching another team!
COACH

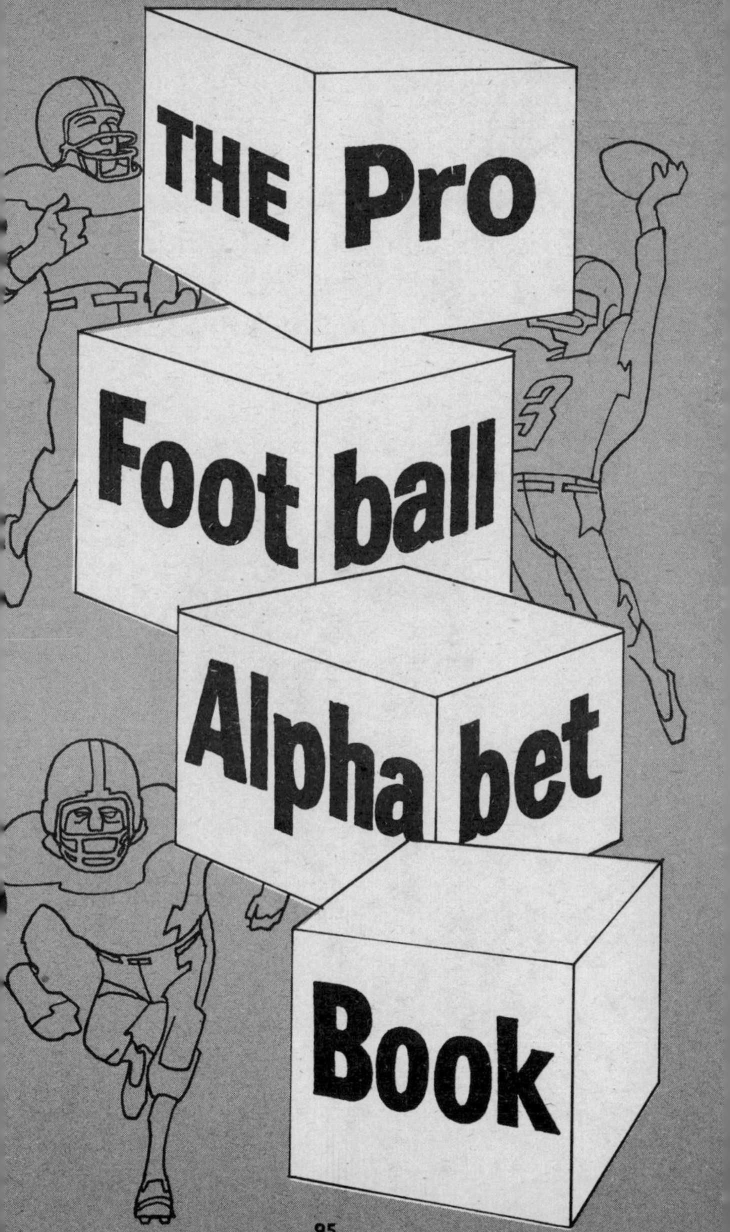
THE Pro
Foot ball
Alpha bet
Book

A is for Announcers —
They add lots of color
In hopes you won't notice
The game's getting duller.

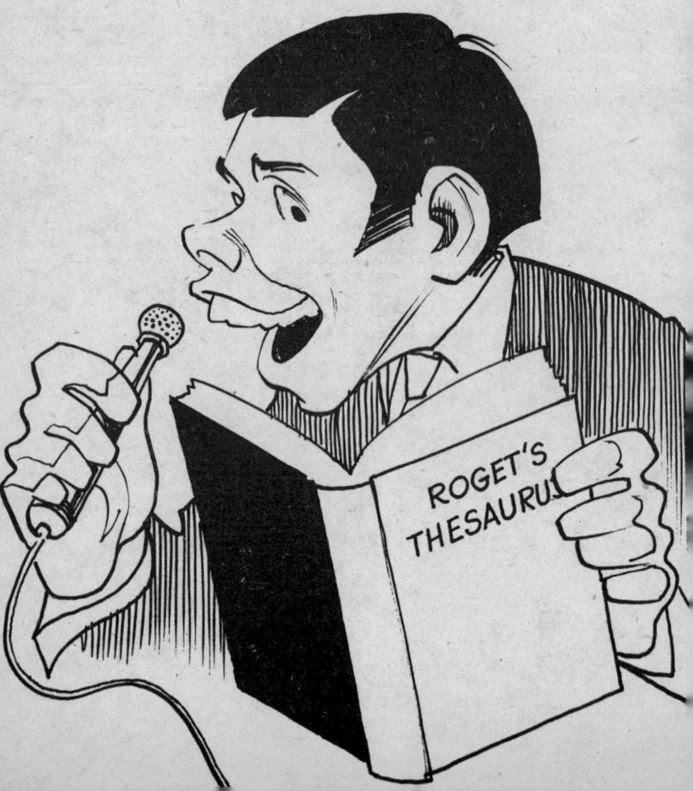
ROGET'S
THESAURU

B is for Bomb,
Which goes through the hands
Of three deep receivers
And into the stands.

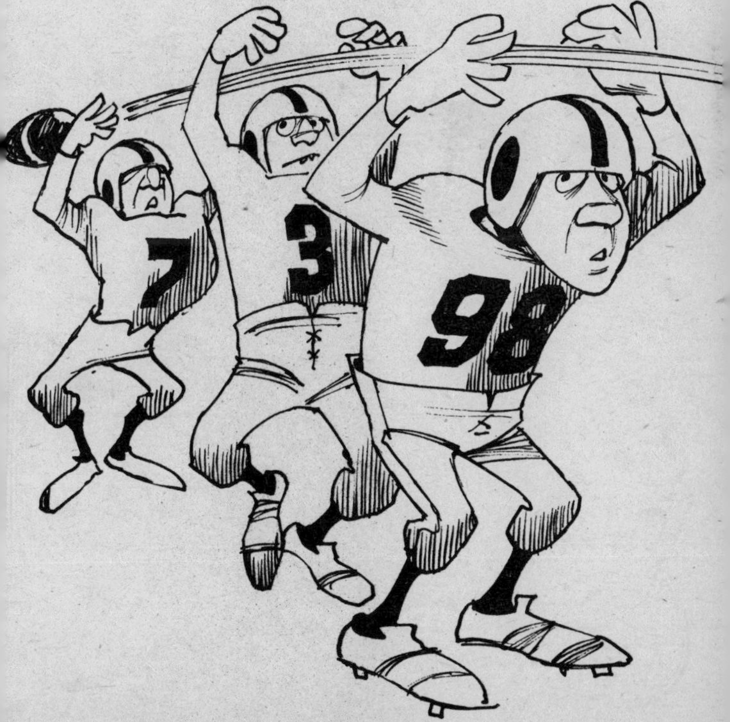
7
3
98

C is for Coach,
Who with anger is burning
On learning his tight end
Gets twice what *he's* earning.

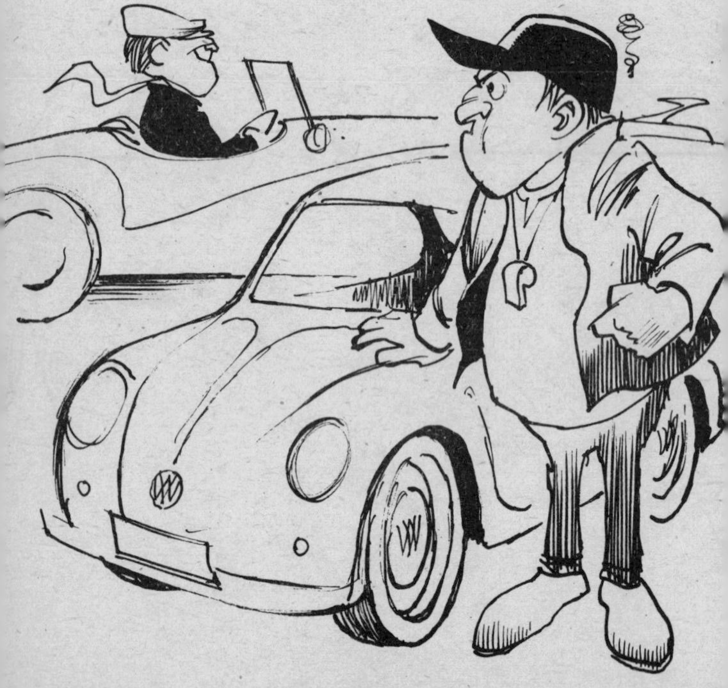

D

is for Defensive Tackle
Who's cheered each time he
Commits dirty fouls
The officials don't see.

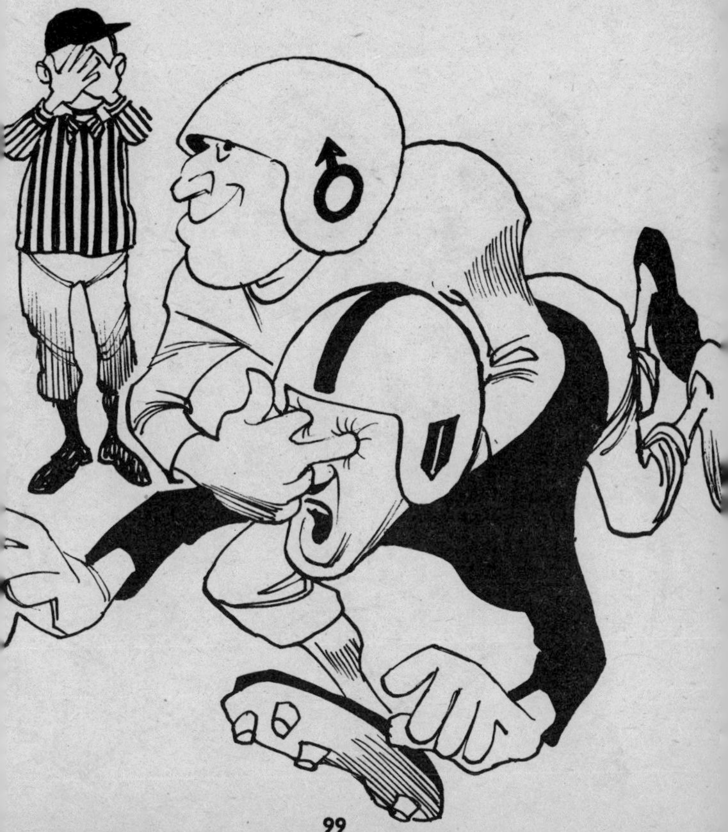

E is for Endorsements
Pros give on the side
To sell all those products
Not one of them's tried.

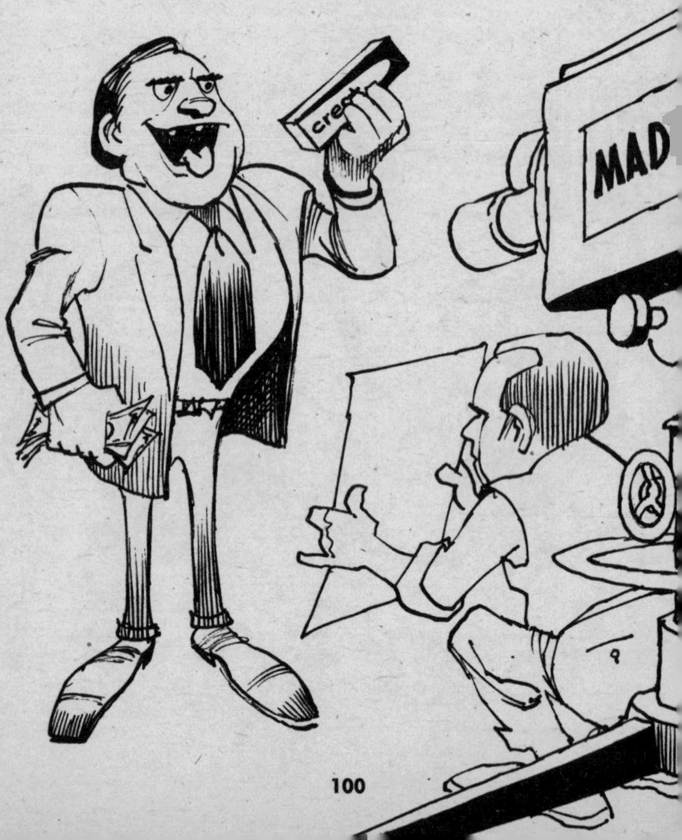
MAD

F

is for First Year Man,
Who runs with great ease;
He's easy to spot —
He's still got two good knees.

G is for Game Plan
The coach says he'll win with;
This usually means
There's no hope to begin with.

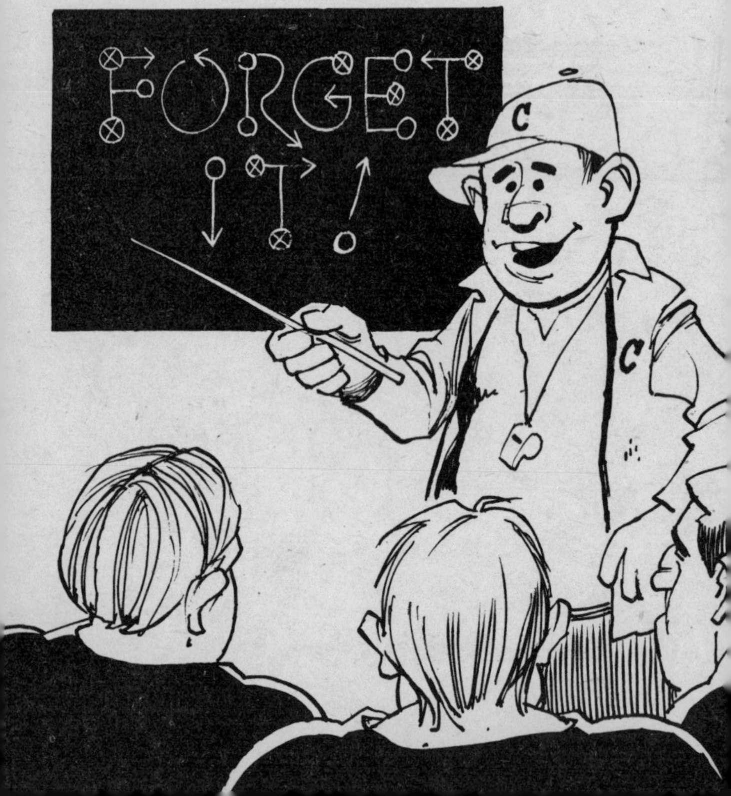
FORGET
IT!

H is for Half a Yard,
The distance it takes
For that crucial first down
That your team never makes.

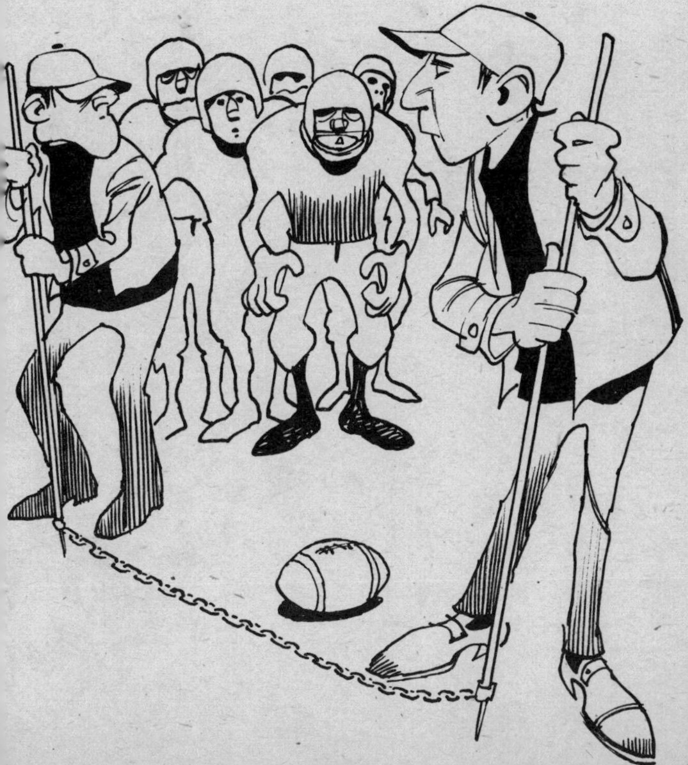

I

is for Injury —
Just hear the fans cheer!
The enemy quarterback's
Lost for the year!

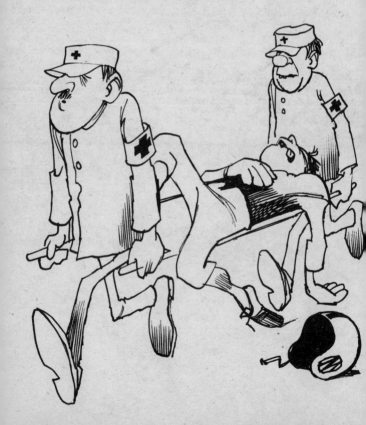

J is for Jet Lag,
Which travel induces;
In case of a loss,
It's the best of excuses.

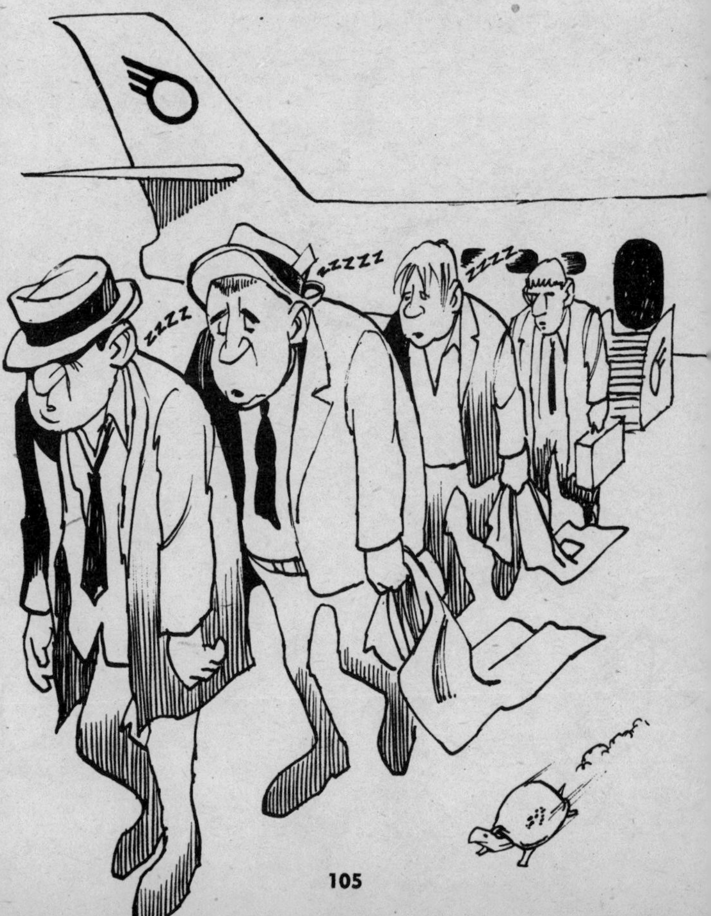
ZZZZ
ZZZZZ
ZZZZ

K is for Kick Returner,
The masochist's idol —
A great way to live
If you feel suicidal.

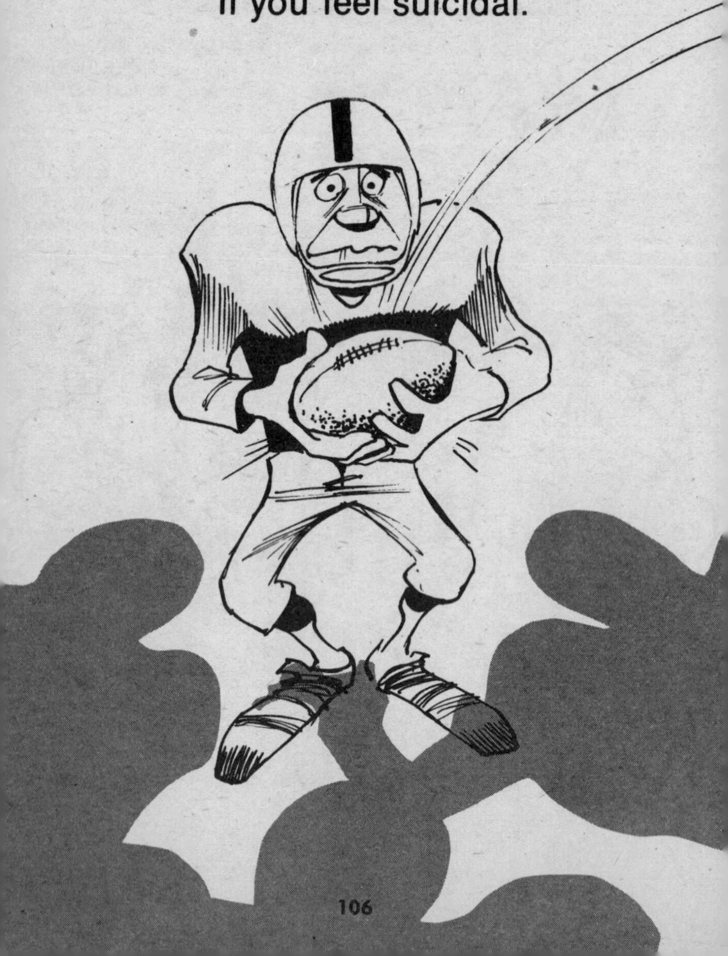

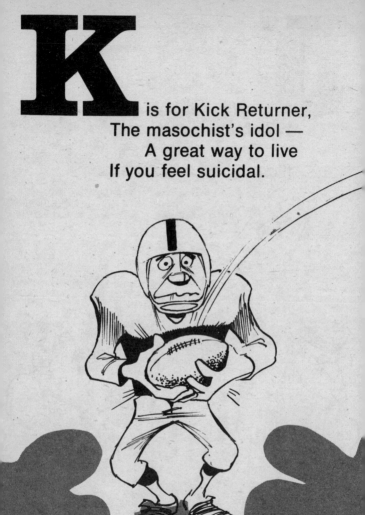

L is for Linebacker —
A great, massive creature;
You've seen him before —
In a Frankenstein feature.

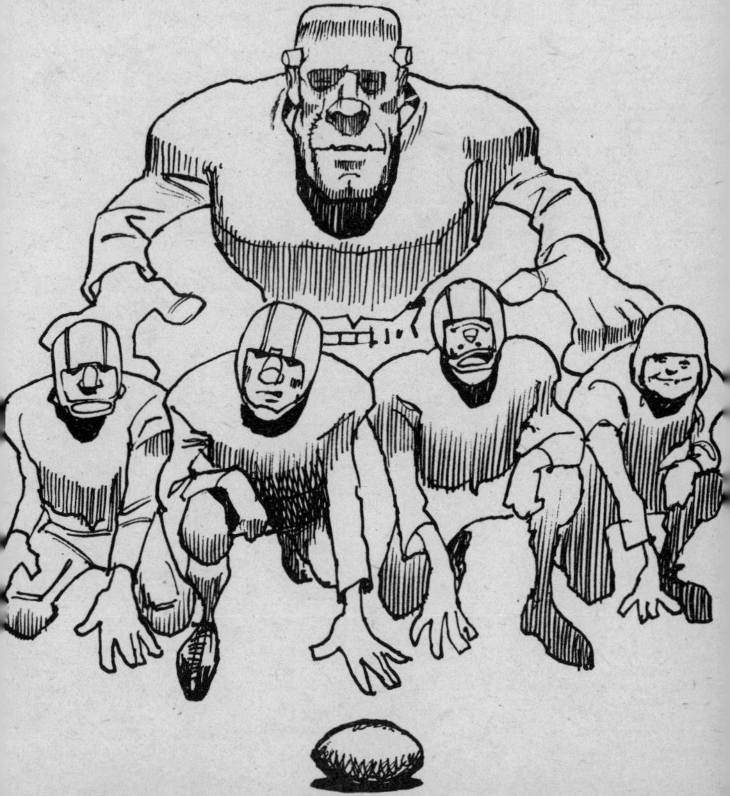

M is for Majorette —
Her twirling is shoddy;
So what? We're all grooving
Her fabulous body.

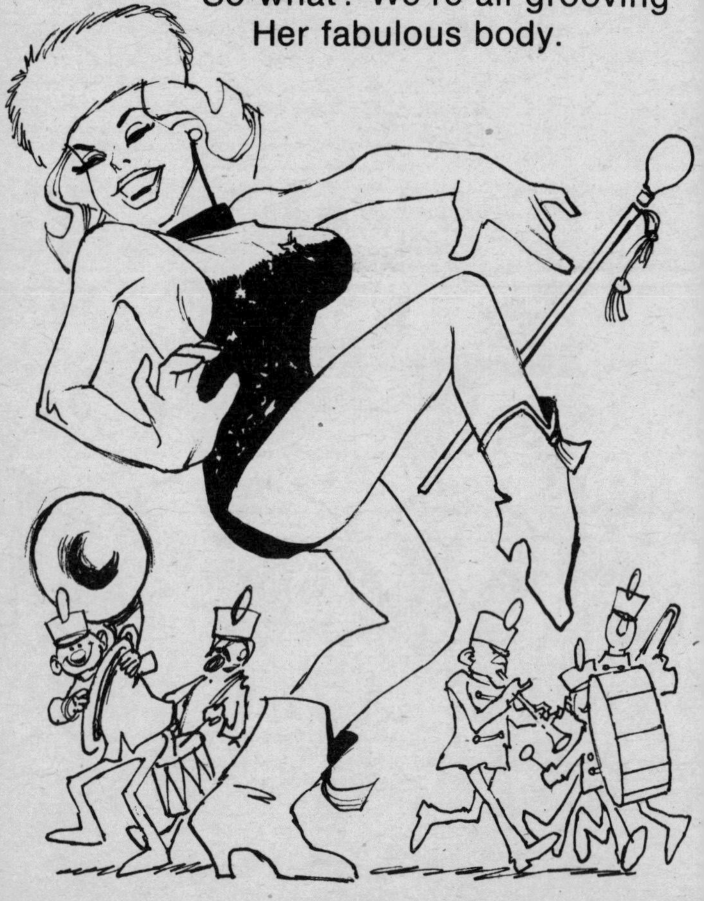

N is for Nice Guy,
Who plays the game clean;
It's been 20 years
Since the last one was seen.

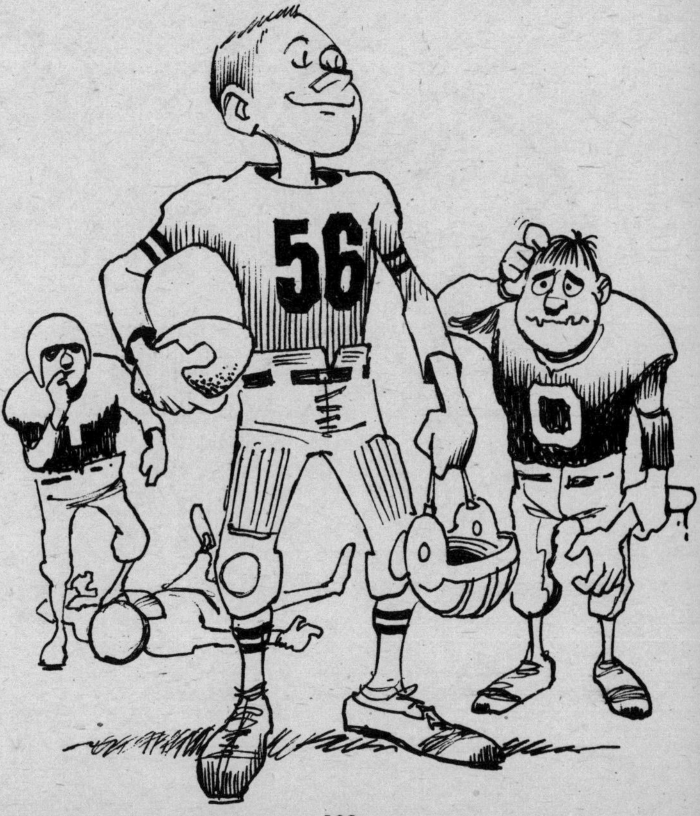
56

O is for Offside —
The ref calls each one
To wipe out the thrill
Of a long touchdown run.

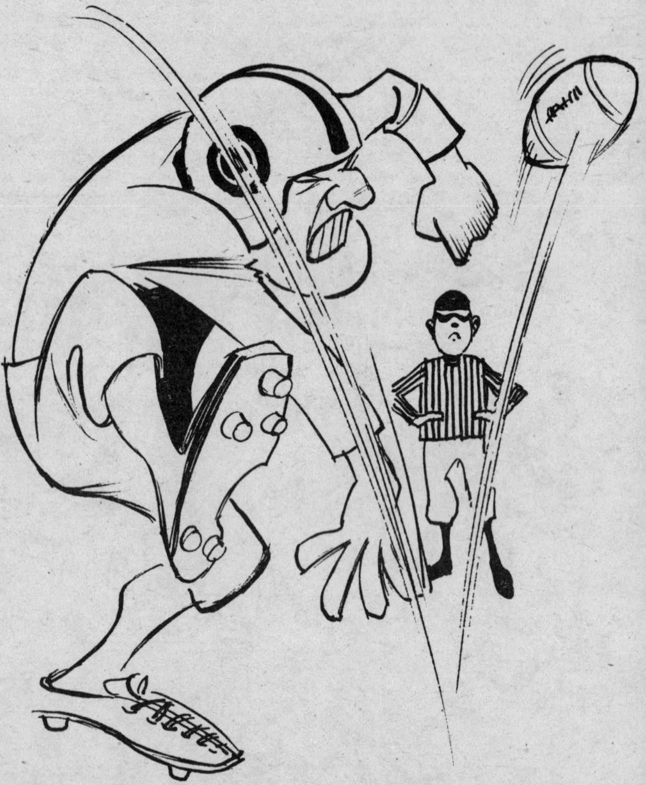

P

is for Pep-talk
The coach gives a player;
They'd both help their cause
If they tried a small prayer.

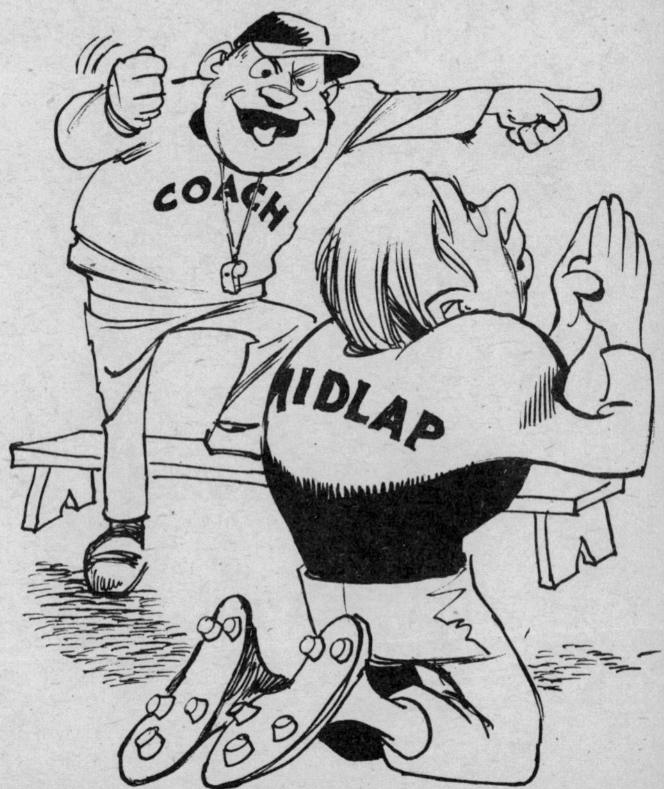
COACH
IDLAP

Q is for Quarterback —
To find him's not hard;
He's there 'neath a tackle,
Two ends and a guard.

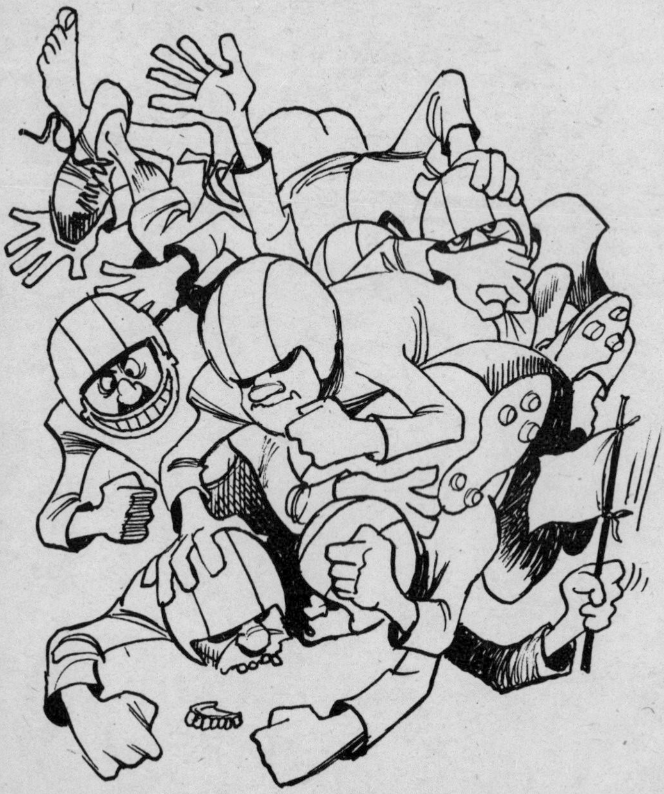

R is for Rain
Which can turn fields to mud;
Still it's helpful for washing
Away the spilled blood.

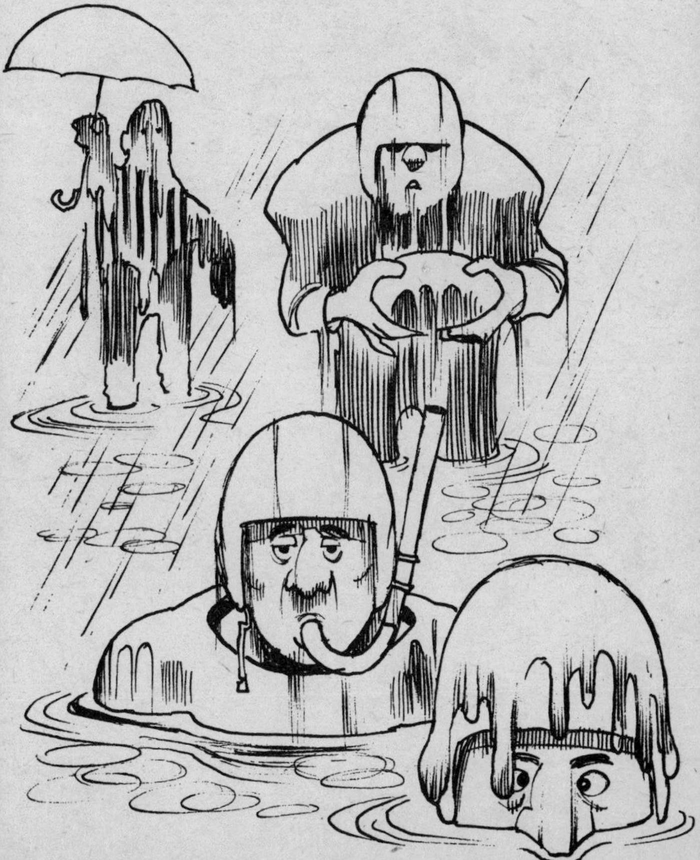

S is for Special Strategy
That coaches all use —
It states, “Get the football,
“Score touchdowns, don’t lose.’

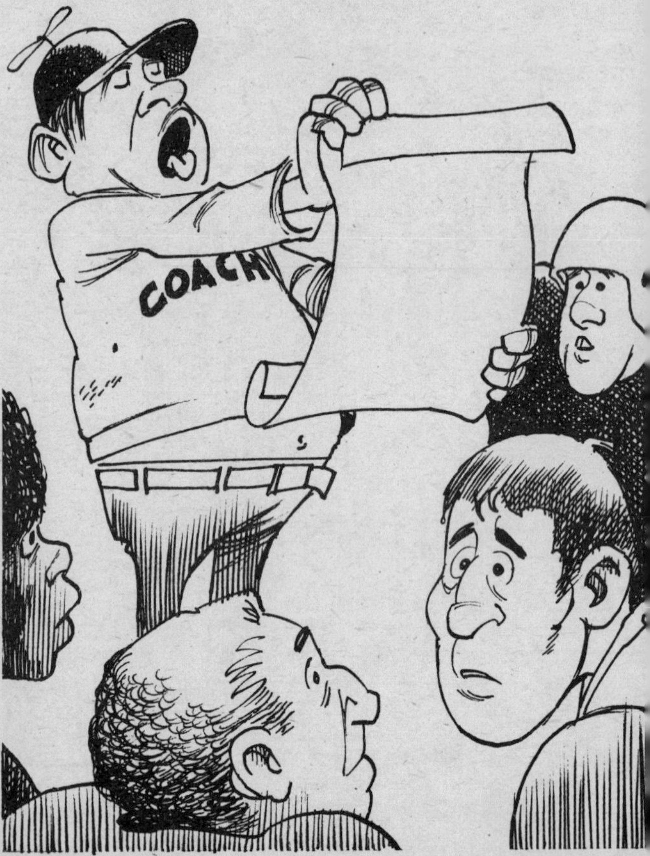
COACH

T is for Trainer,
Whom players acclaim;
His groovy green pills
Get them "up" for the game.

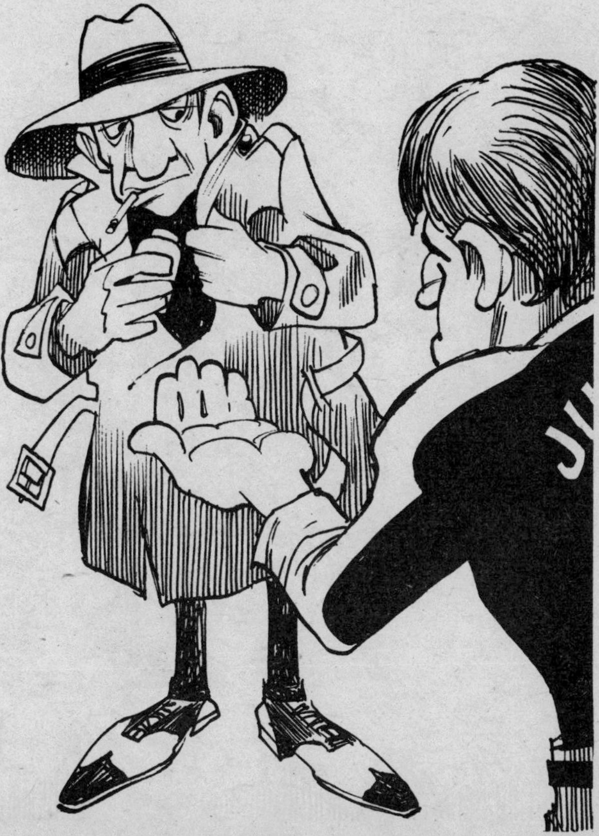

U

is for Upset —
For some flunky reason,
Your team's won its first game —
To close out the season.

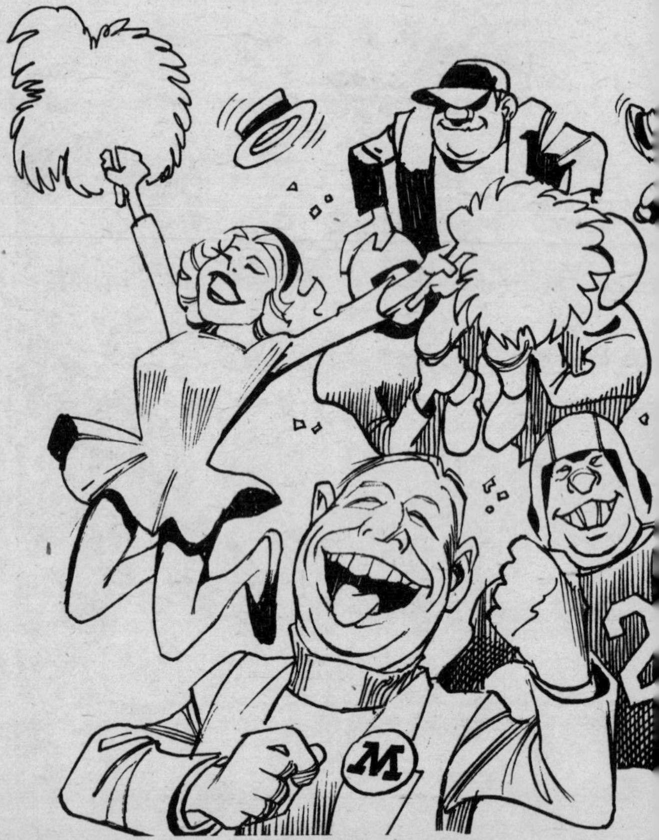

V

is for Volley
We hit on the court;
We draw back our racket —
Oops! Sorry — wrong sport!

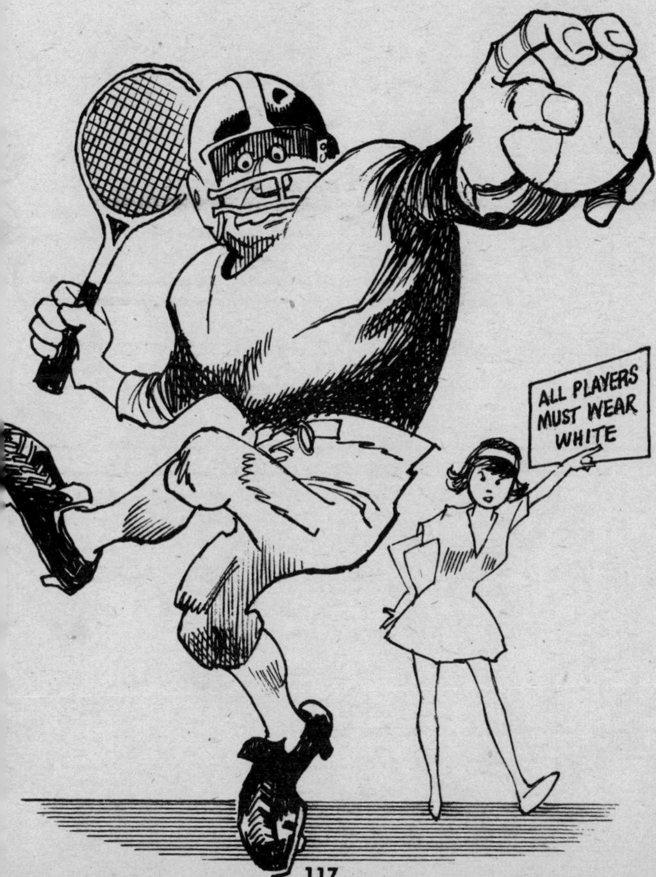
ALL PLAYERS
MUST WEAR
WHITE

W is for Workouts,
Which start every Monday,
Perfecting the plays
That are loused up on Sunday.

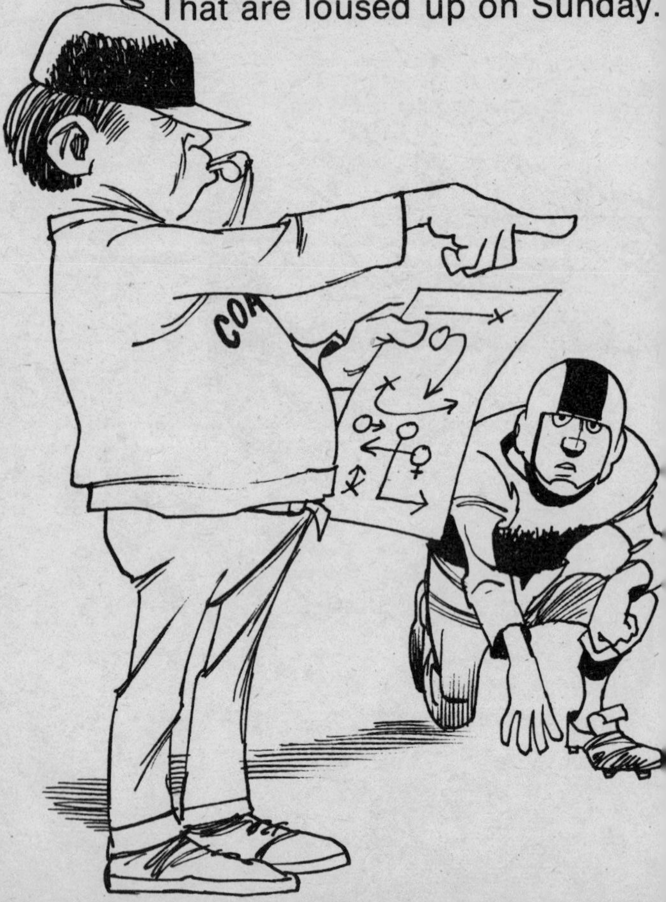

X is for X-tra Point Try —
A time of great tension,
Which has all the thrills
Of a dentists convention.

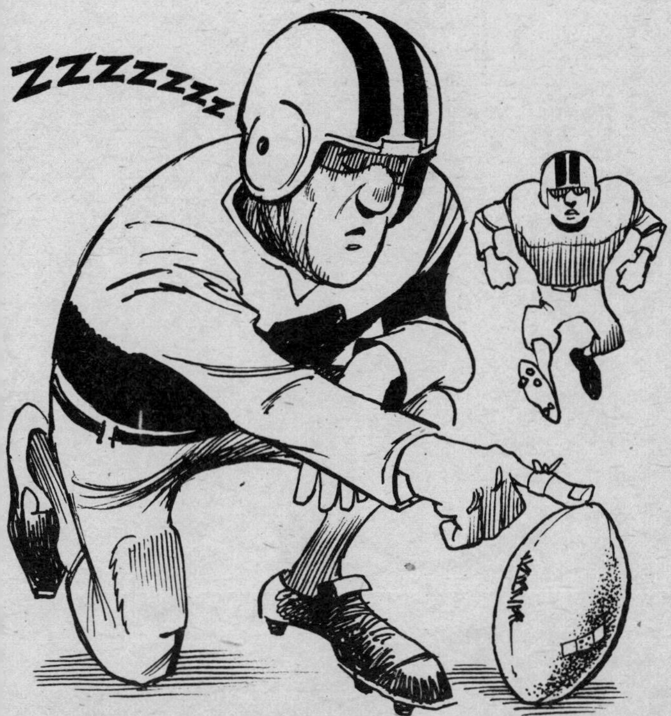
ZZZZZZzz

Y is for Yards Gained,
Which makes rooters cheer;
Your team's gained 500 —
But that's for the year.

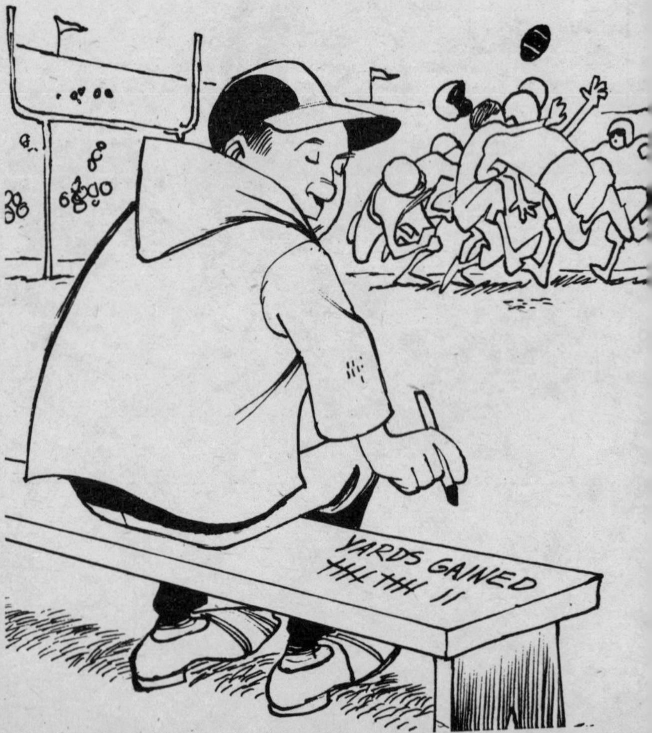
YARDS GAINED

Z is for Zeros
Up there on the scoreboard;
Just wait till next season —
You're sure to be more bored.

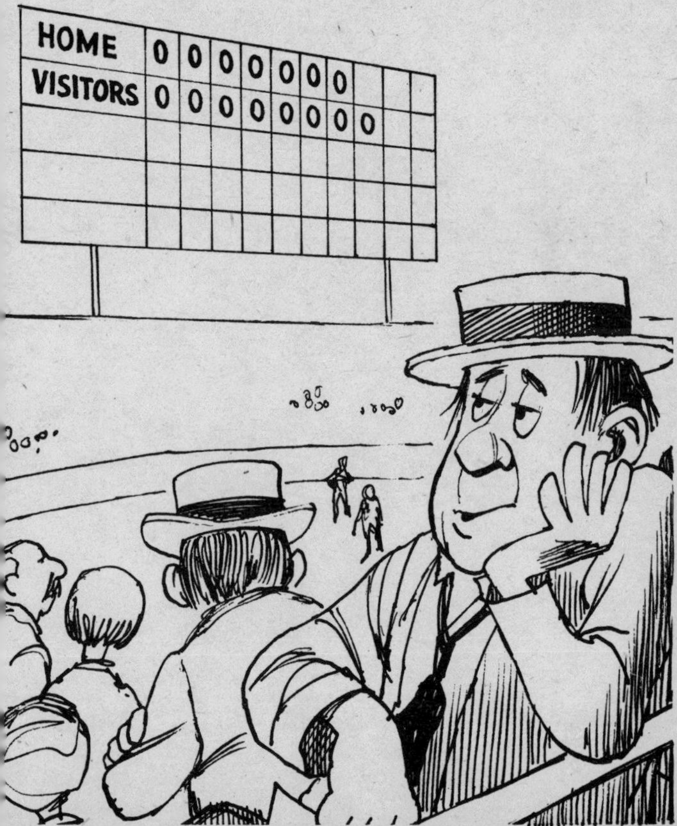
HOME 0 0 0 0 0 0 0
VISITORS 0 0 0 0 0 0 0 0

SPORTS

M ADDITIONS

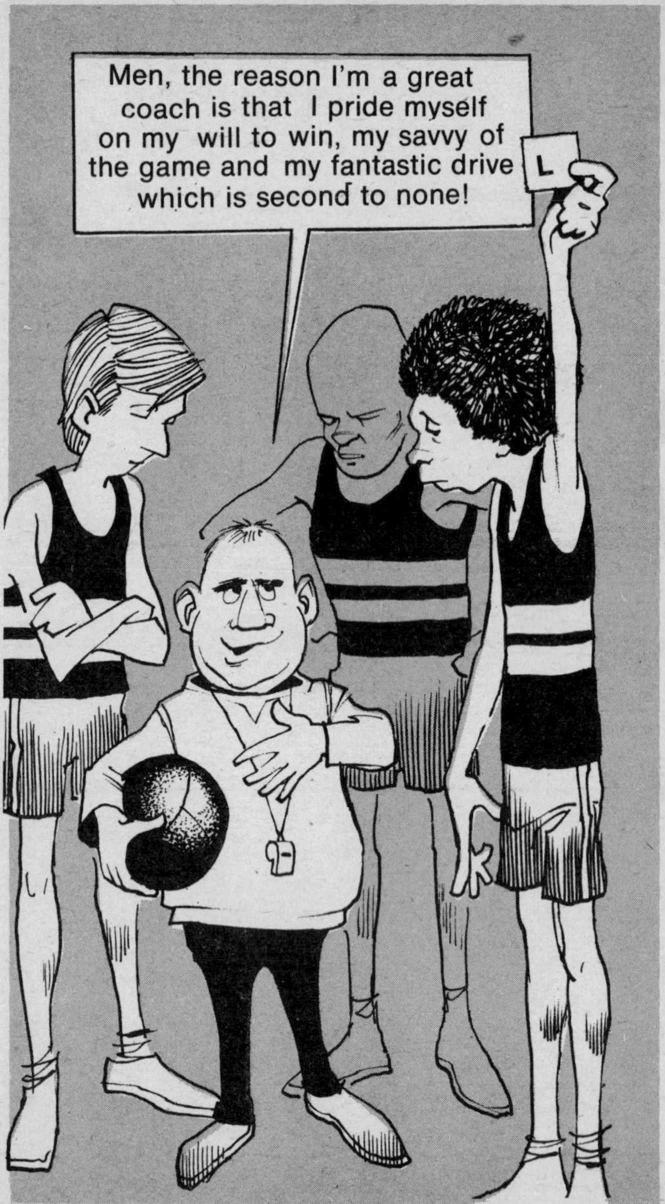
Men, the reason I'm a great coach is that I pride myself on my will to win, my savvy of the game and my fantastic drive which is second to none!
L

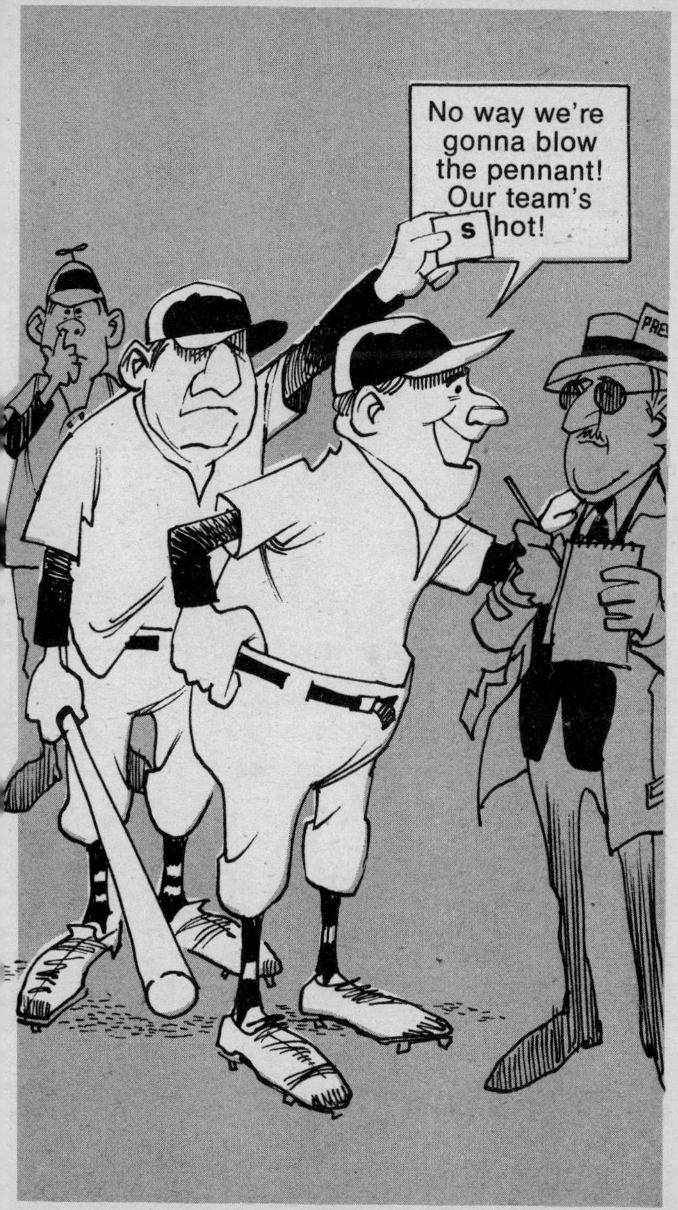
No way we're gonna blow the pennant! Our team's s hot!
PRES

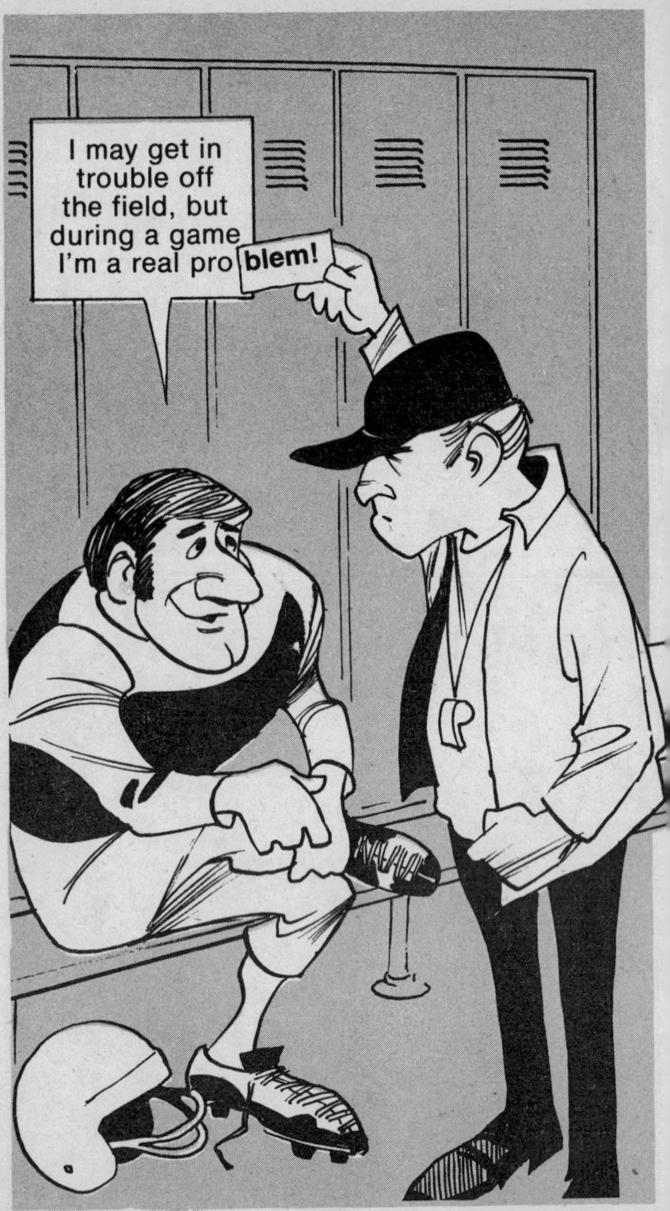
I may get in trouble off the field, but during a game I'm a real pro
blem!

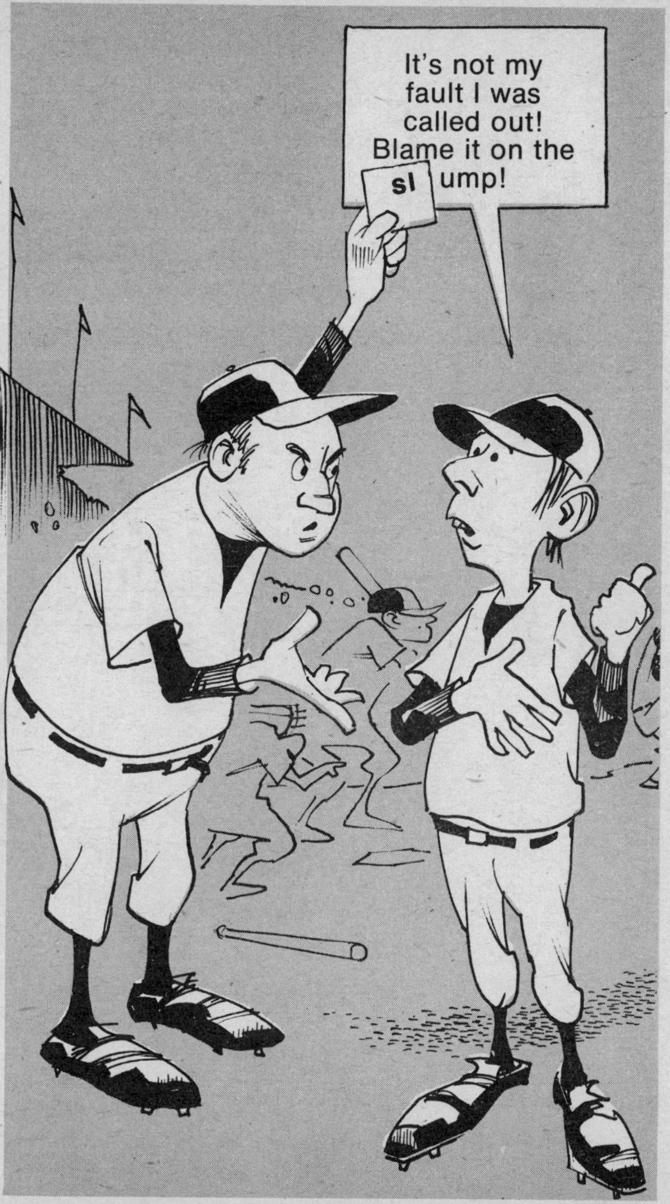
It's not my fault I was called out! Blame it on the
sl
ump!

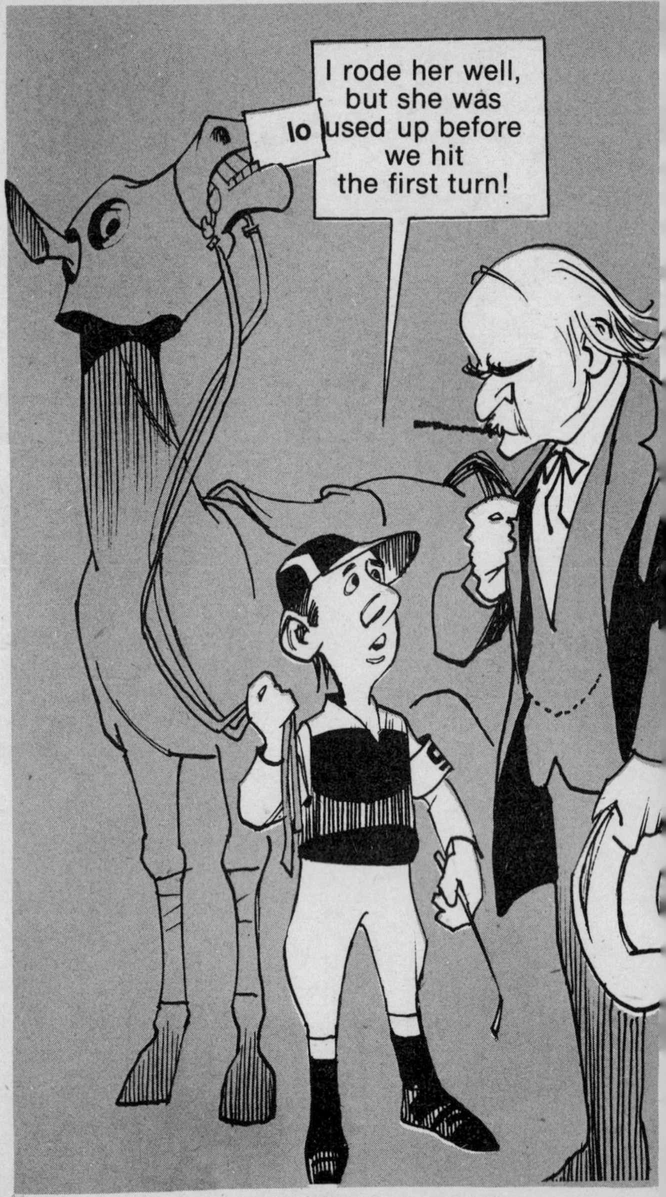
lo
I rode her well, but she was used up before we hit the first turn!

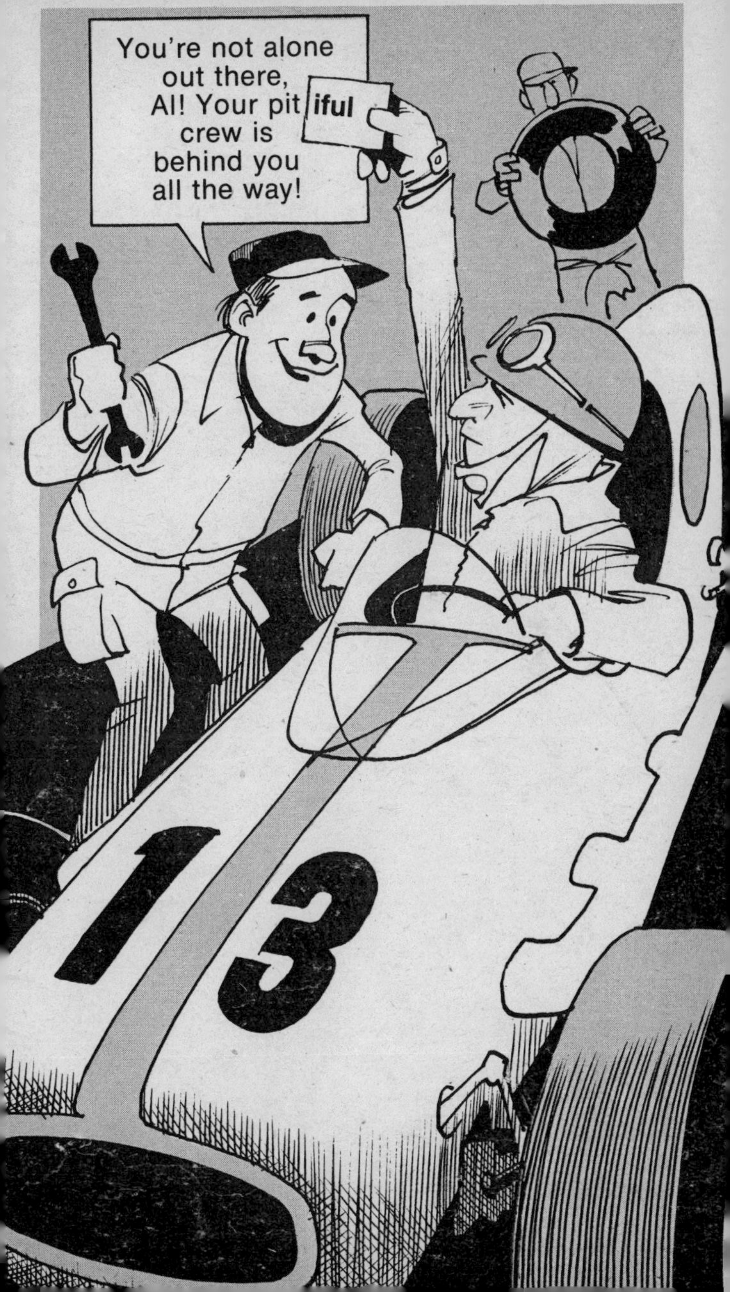
You're not alone out there, Al! Your pit iful crew is behind you all the way!
13

You know your Playing Days are Numbered when...

You know your playing days are numbered. . .

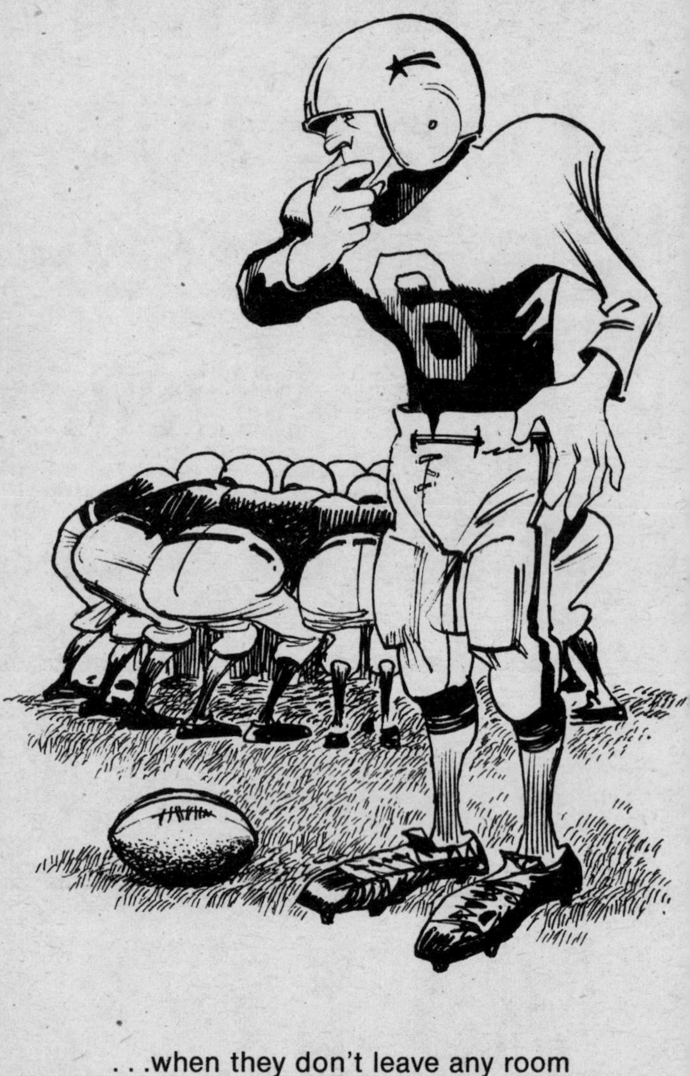

. . .when they don't leave any room for you in the huddle.

You know your playing days are numbered. . .

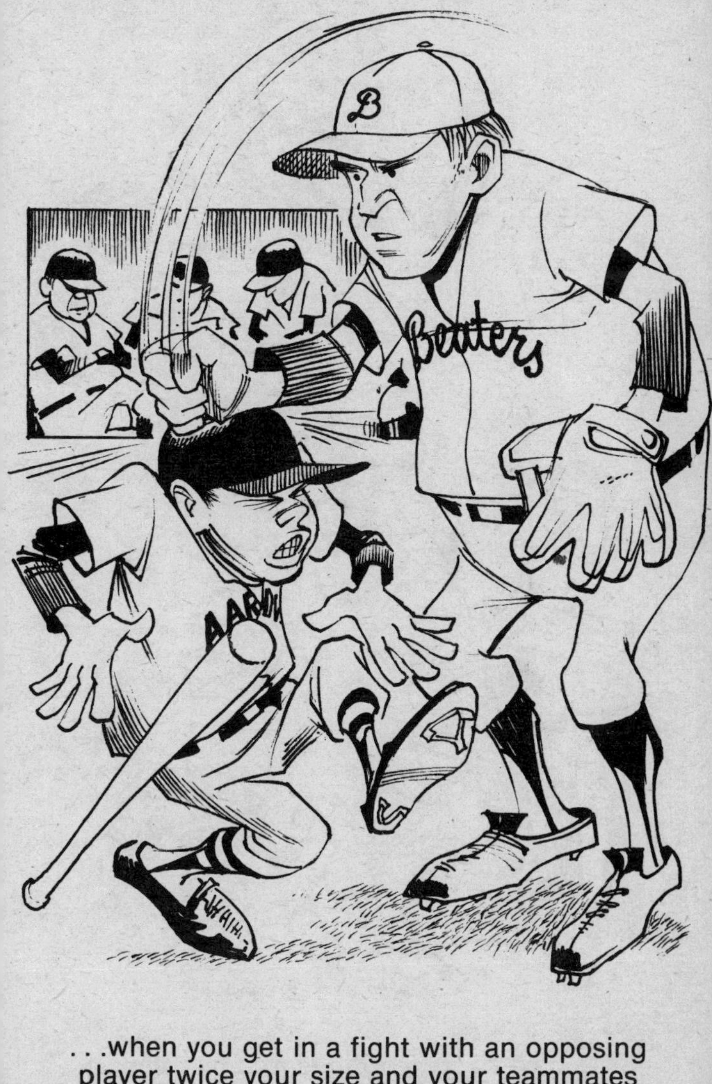

B
Beaters

. . .when you get in a fight with an opposing player twice your size and your teammates stay in the dugout.

You know your playing days are numbered. . .

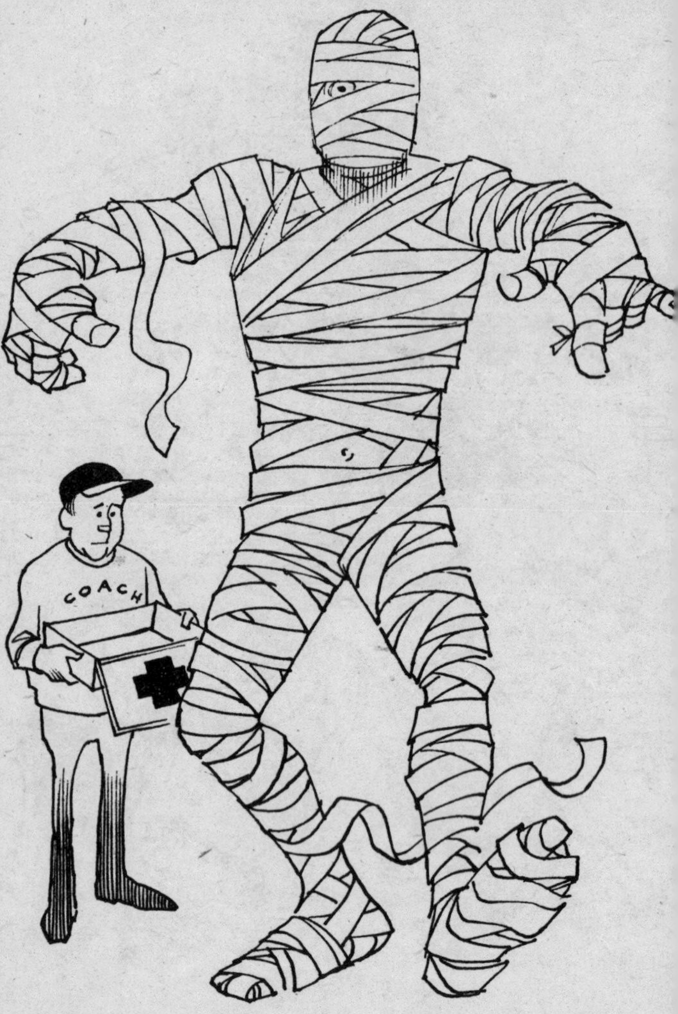
COACH

. . .when there's more of your body taped up than not taped up.

You know your playing days are numbered. . .

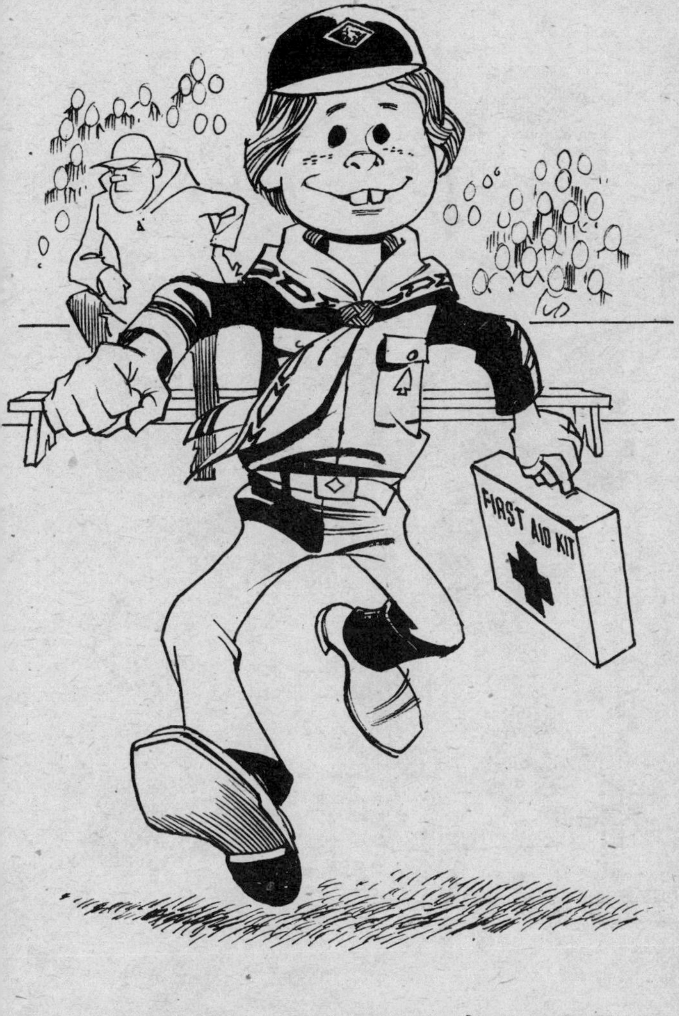
FIRST AID KIT

. . .when you're lying unconscious on the field and the trainer sends out his assistant to look you over.

You know your playing days are numbered. . .

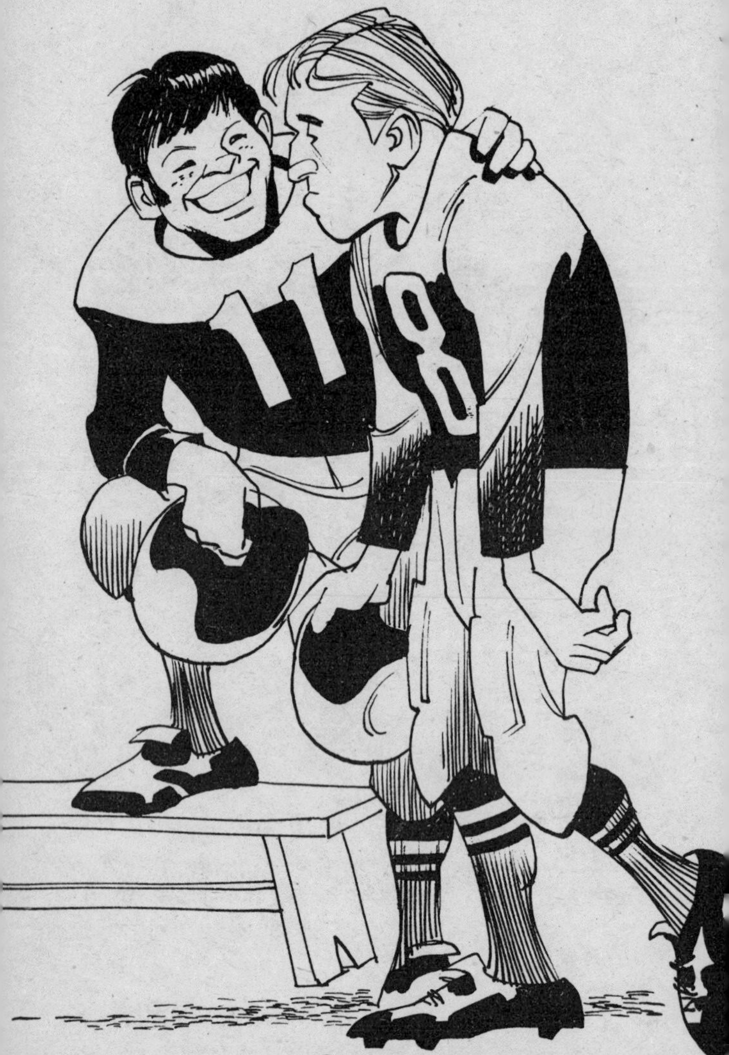

. . .when the younger players call you "Pops."

You know your playing days are numbered. . .

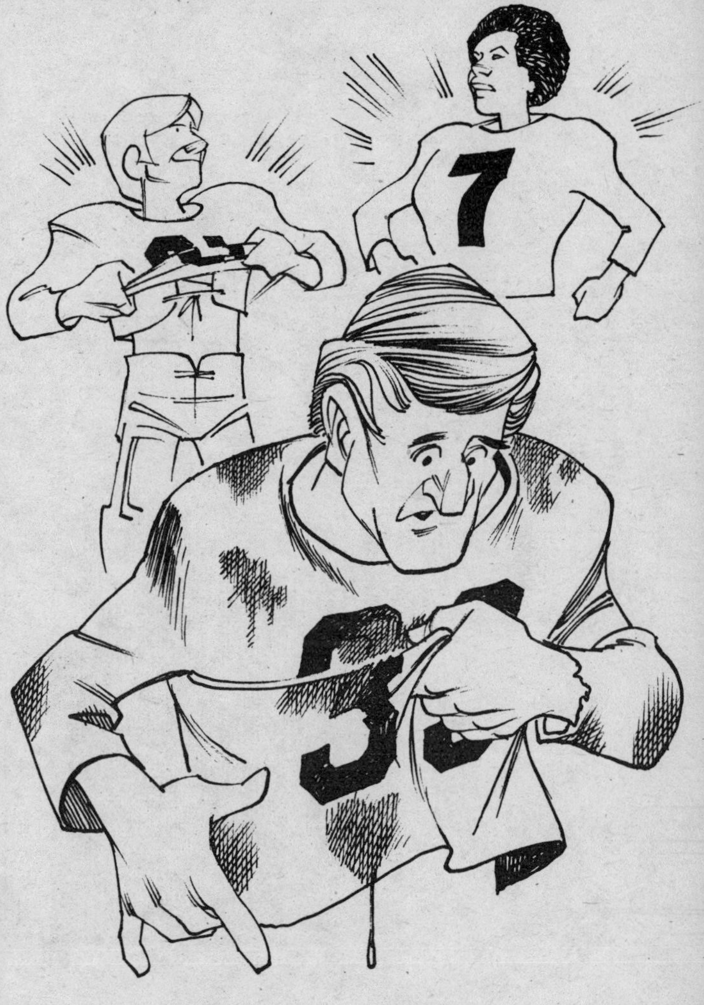
7

. . .when the team suits up before a game and you realize yours is the only uniform that hasn't been laundered.

You know your playing days are numbered. . .

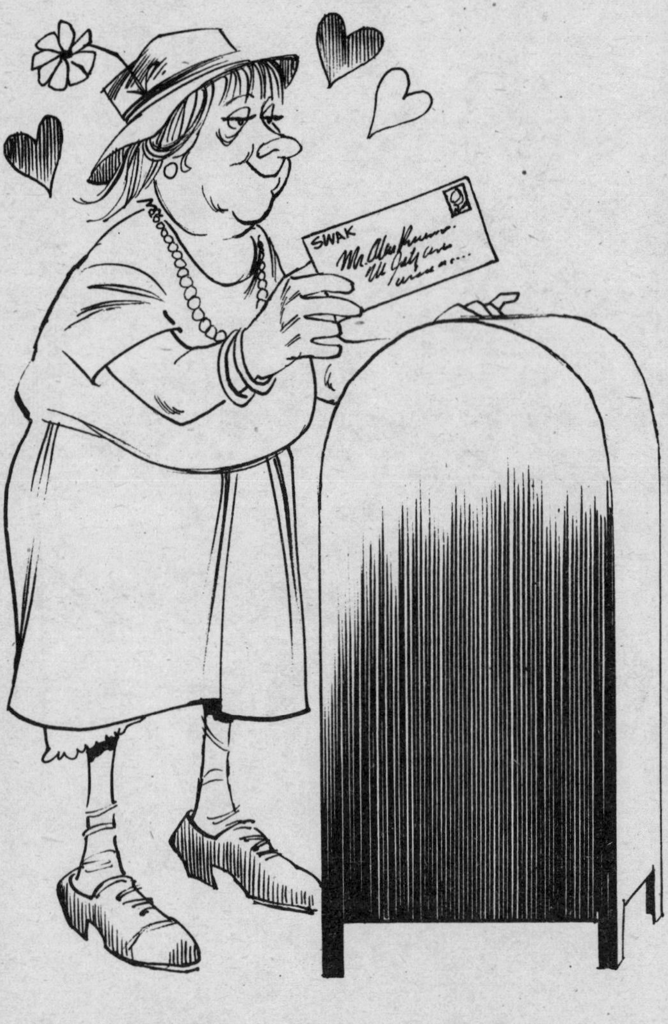
SWAK

. . .when your fan-mail consists mostly of letters from middle-aged women.

You know your playing days are numbered. . .

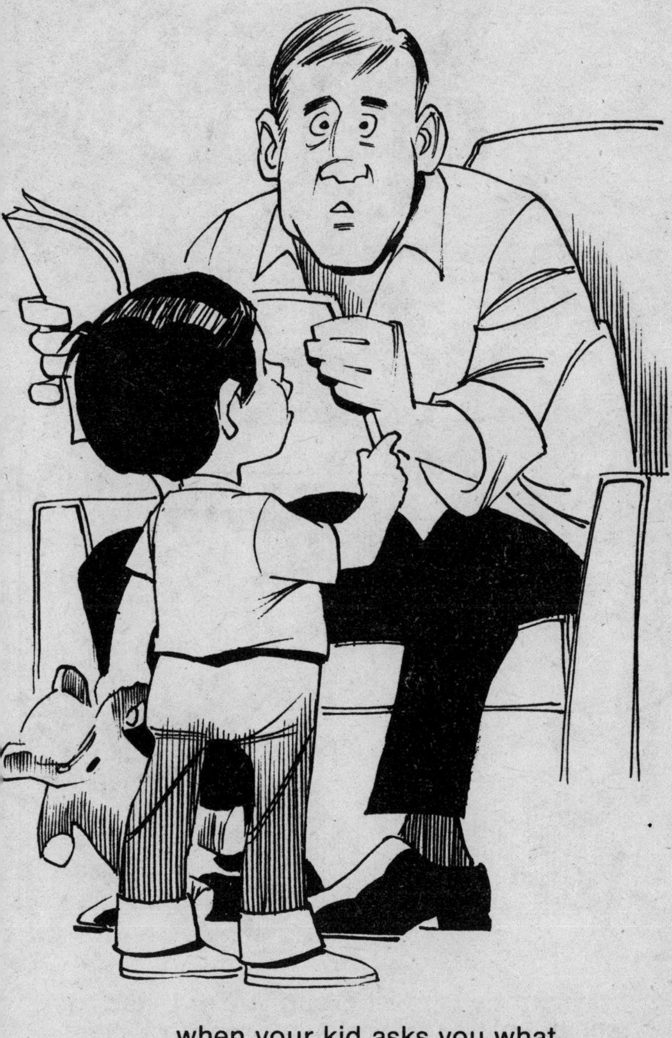

. . .when your kid asks you what you do for a living.

You know your playing days are numbered. . .

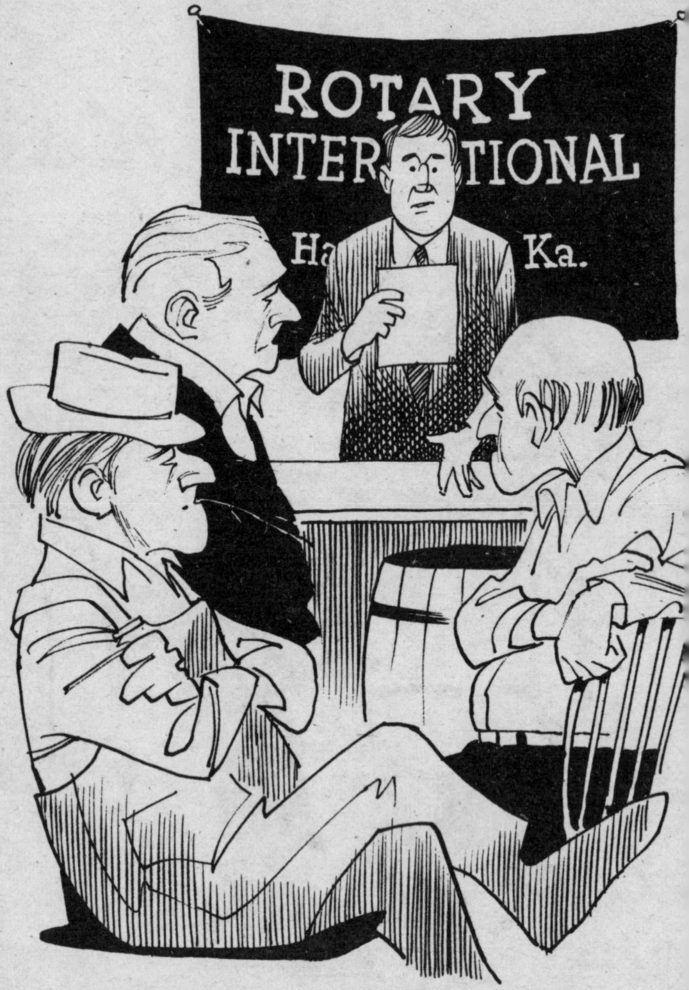
ROTARY
INTER TIONAL
Ha Ka.

. . .when the biggest group you're asked to speak before during the off-season is the Hayes Center, Kansas, Rotary Club.

You know your playing days are numbered. . .

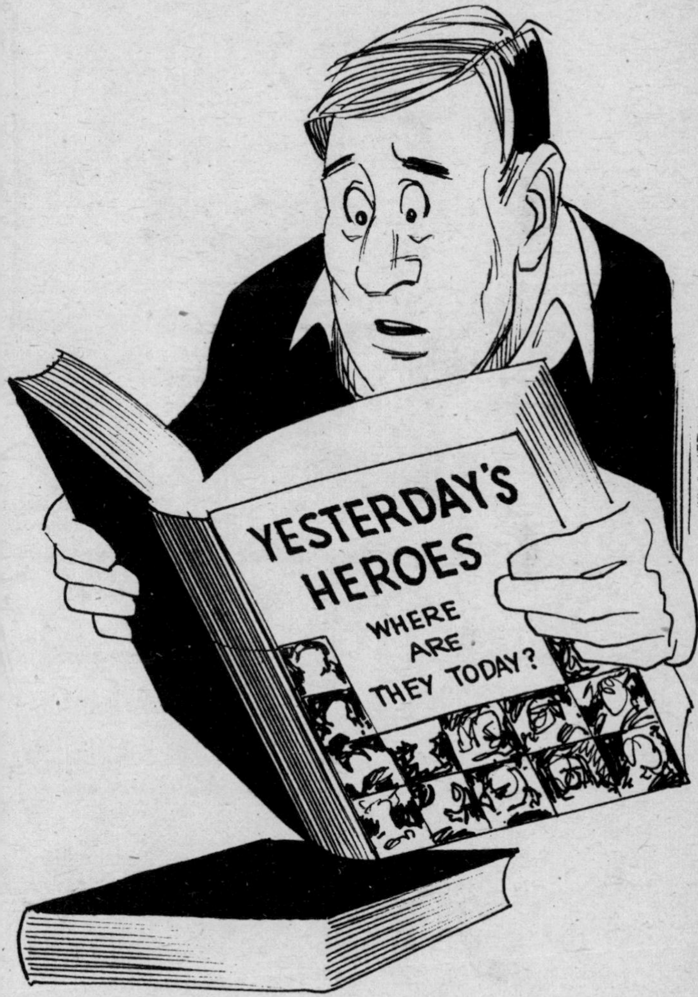
YESTERDAY'S HEROES
WHERE ARE THEY TODAY?

. . .when you find your photo in a "Where Are They Now?" book.

You know your playing days are numbered. . .

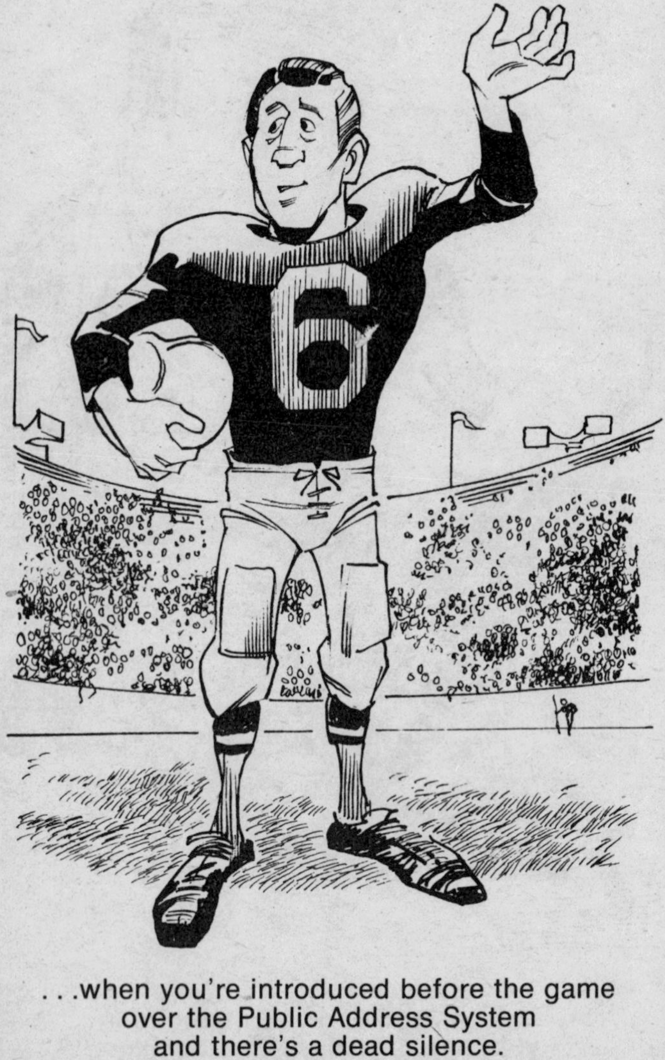

. . .when you're introduced before the game over the Public Address System and there's a dead silence.

You know your playing days are numbered. . .

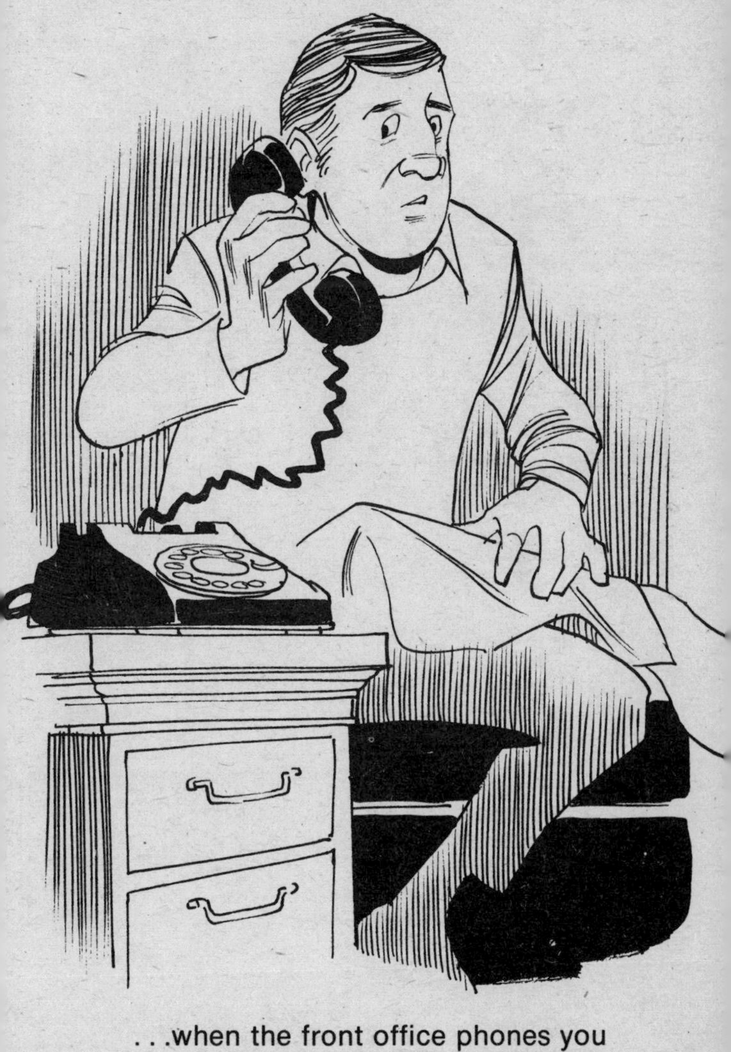

. . .when the front office phones you about your contract for the coming year and the call comes in collect.

You know your playing days are numbered. . .

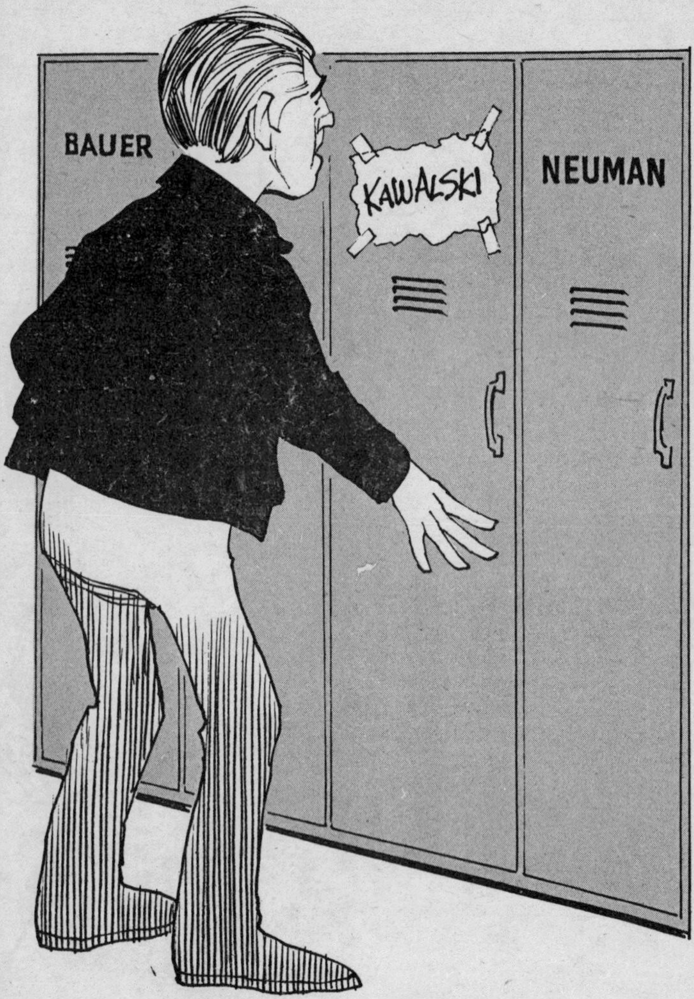
BAUER
KAWALSKI
NEUMAN

. . .when your name on your locker is scrawled on a piece of scratch paper and Scotch-taped for easy removal.

You know your playing days are numbered. . .

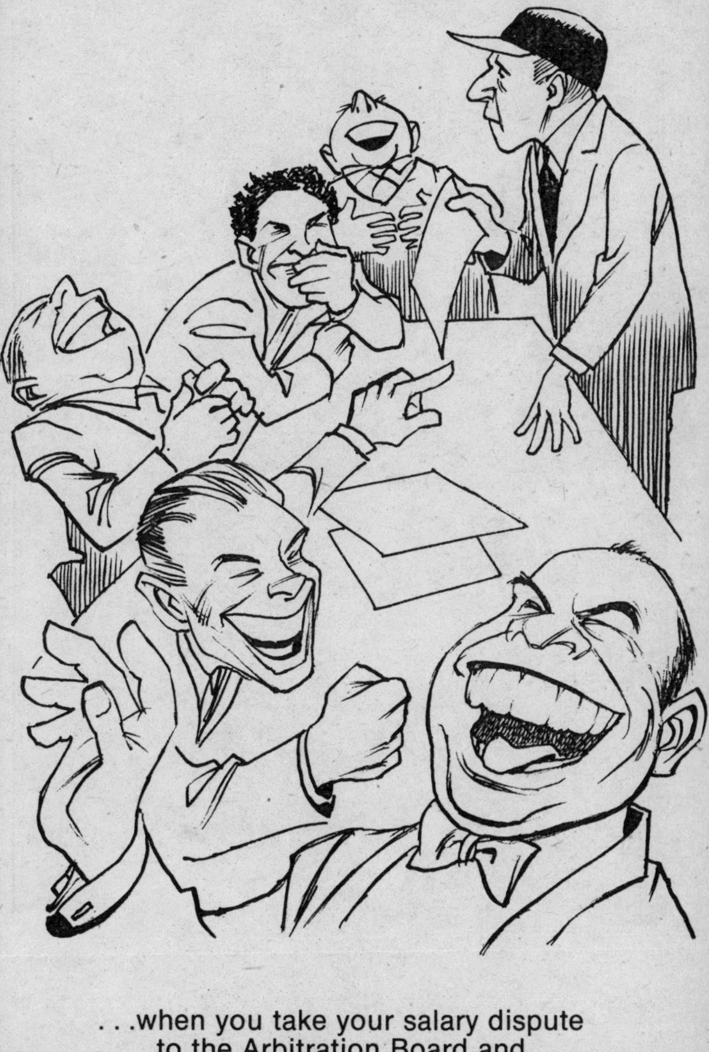

. . .when you take your salary dispute to the Arbitration Board and they laugh in your face.

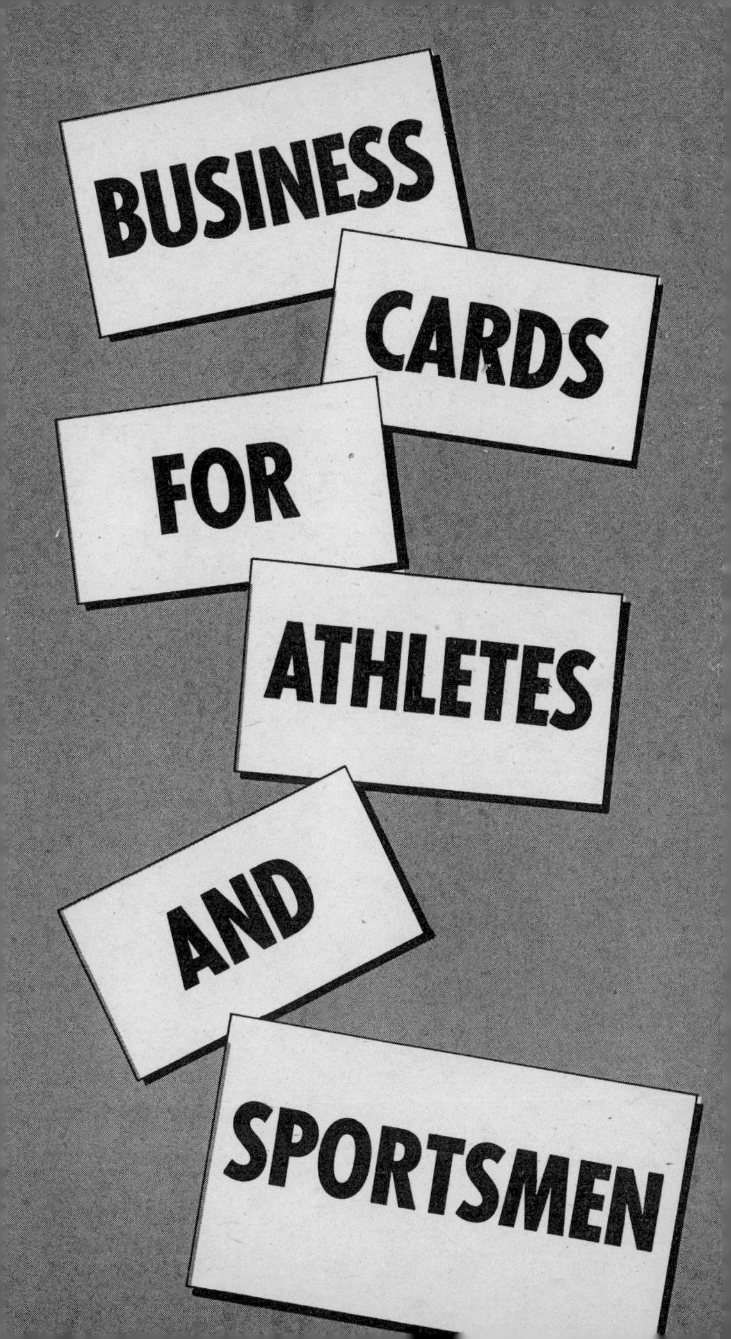
BUSINESS
CARDS
FOR
ATHLETES
AND
SPORTSMEN

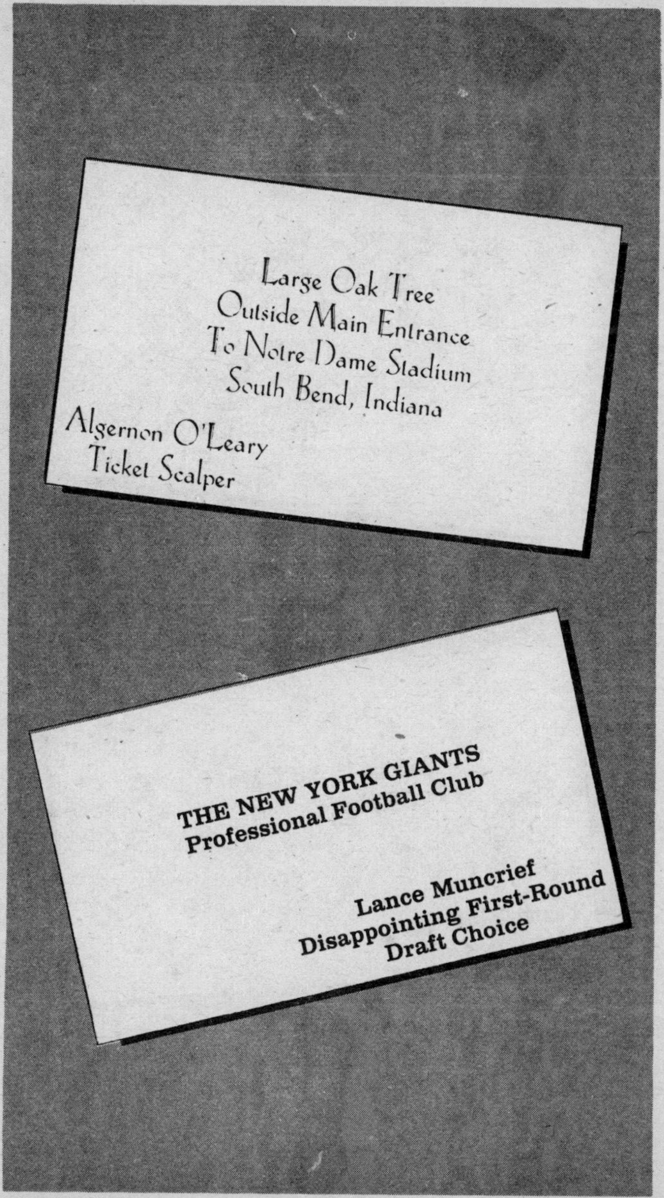
Large Oak Tree
Outside Main Entrance
To Notre Dame Stadium
South Bend, Indiana
Algernon O'Leary
Ticket Scalper
THE NEW YORK GIANTS
Professional Football Club
Lance Muncrief
Disappointing First-Round
Draft Choice

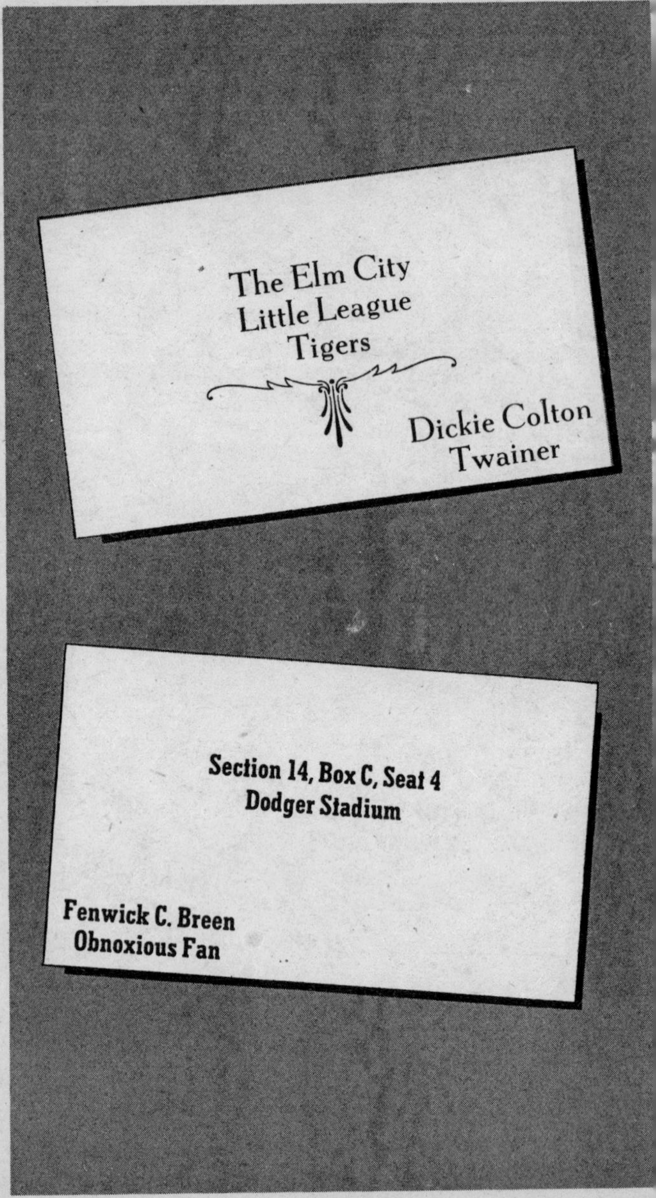
The Elm City
Little League
Tigers
Dickie Colton
Twainer
Section 14, Box C, Seat 4
Dodger Stadium
Fenwick C. Breen
Obnoxious Fan

Office Of The General Manager
Chicago Bulls
Professional Basketball Club

Arthur T. Slade
Front Office Creep

The St. Louis Cardinals
Professional Baseball Club

Miss Wanda LaFleur
Team Follower
And Morale Booster

THE ATLANTA BRAVES
Professional Baseball Club

Clyde Twitty
Run-Of-The-Mill Shortstop

Grogan's Drugstore
Moline, Illinois

Albert Esterhazy III
Pinball Freak

THE GREEN BAY PACKERS
PROFESSIONAL FOOTBALL CLUB

Robert "Monk" Winchester
All-League Dirty Player

George Washington
Elementary School
Pittsburgh,
Pa.

Marvin Ogilvie
Frisbee Hustler

Back Room
Irv's Candy Store
Second Building From The Corner
On Fourth Street
Between Main And Hudson
Baltimore, Maryland

Monroe "Odds" Grulnik
Friendly Bookie

THE KUNG FU
KARATE SCHOOL

✳ Sidney Chung
Shouting and Grunting

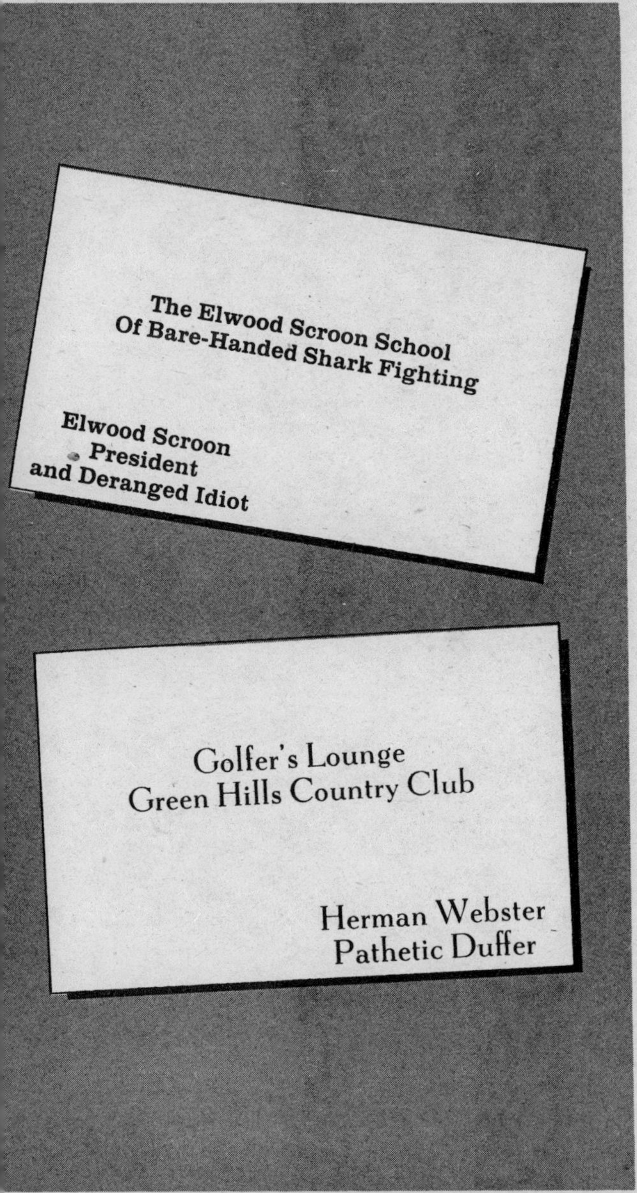
The Elwood Scroon School
Of Bare-Handed Shark Fighting
Elwood Scroon
President
and Deranged Idiot
Golfer's Lounge
Green Hills Country Club
Herman Webster
Pathetic Duffer

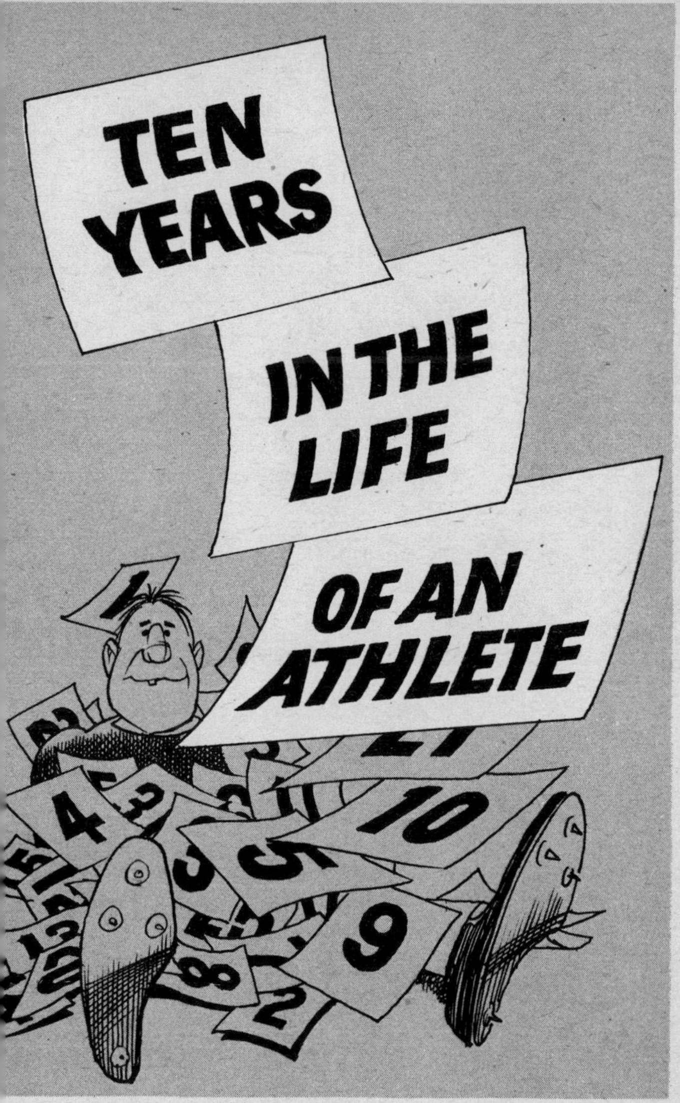
TEN YEARS
IN THE LIFE
OF AN ATHLETE

1971

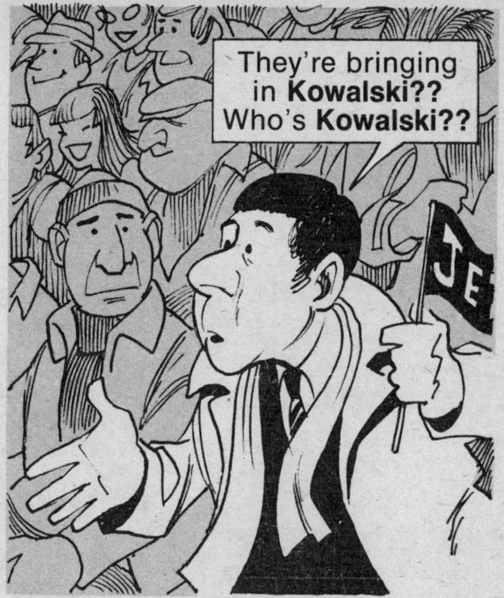
They're bringing in **Kowalski??** Who's **Kowalski??**
JE

1972

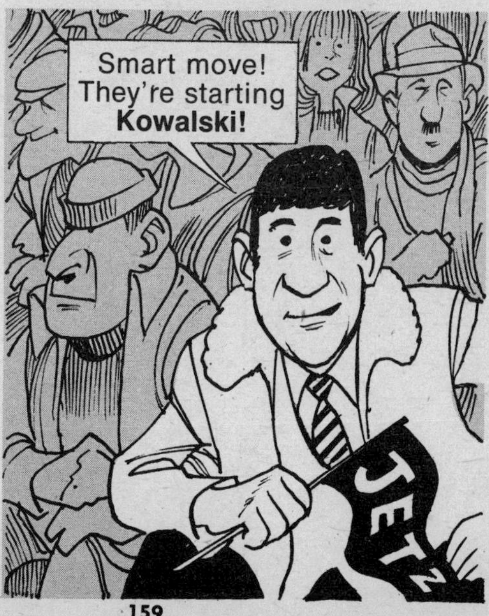
Smart move! They're starting **Kowalski!**
JETZ

1973

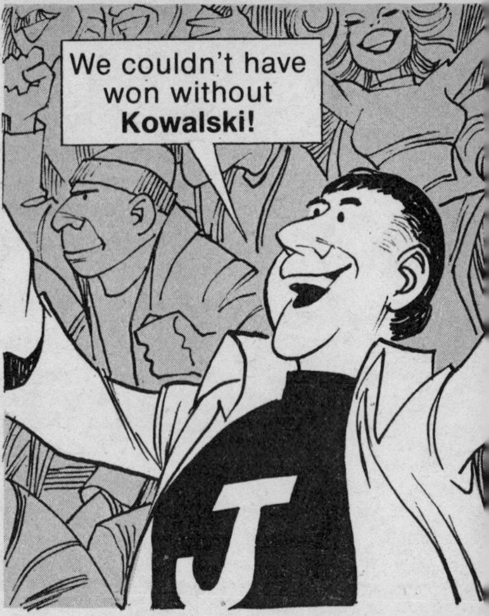
We couldn't have won without **Kowalski!**
J

1974

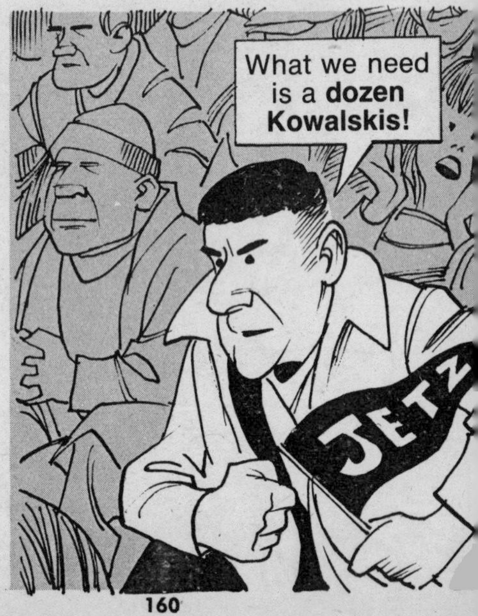
What we need is a **dozen Kowalskis!**
JETZ

1975

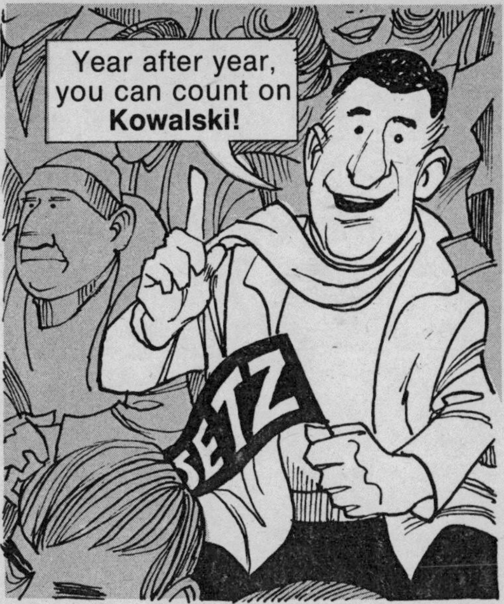
Year after year,
you can count on
Kowalski!

1976

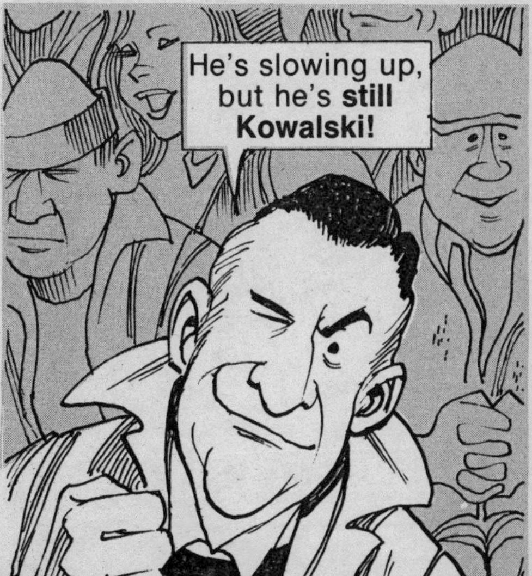
He's slowing up,
but he's **still**
Kowalski!

1977

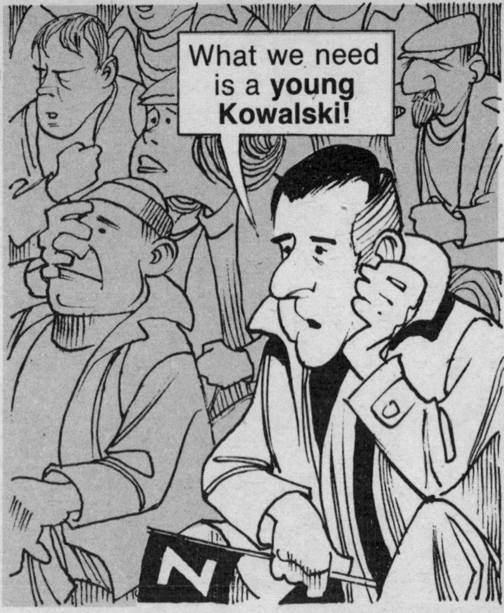

What we need is a **young** **Kowalski!**

1978

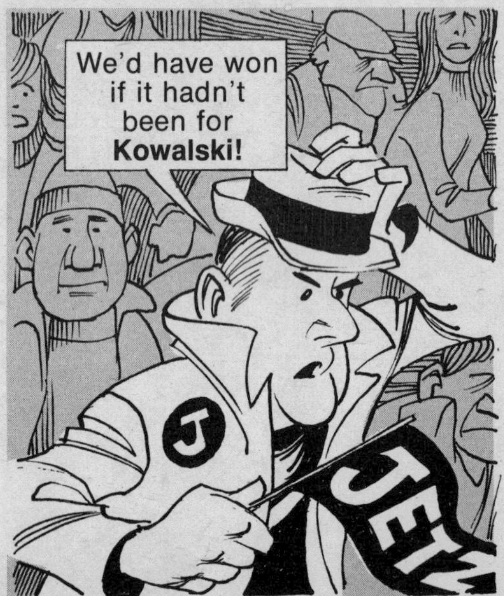

We'd have won if it hadn't been for **Kowalski!**

1979

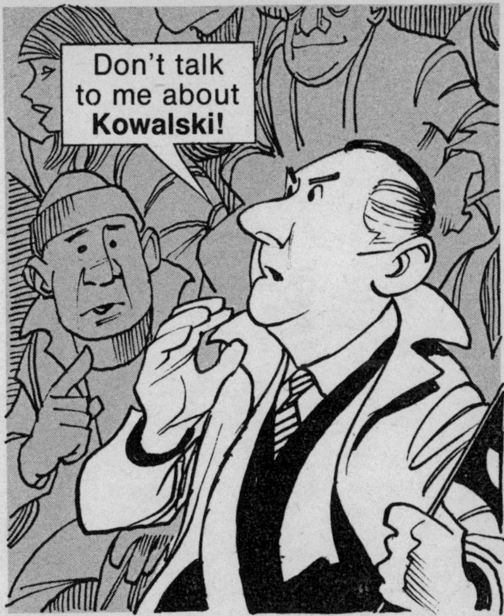
Don't talk to me about **Kowalski!**

1980

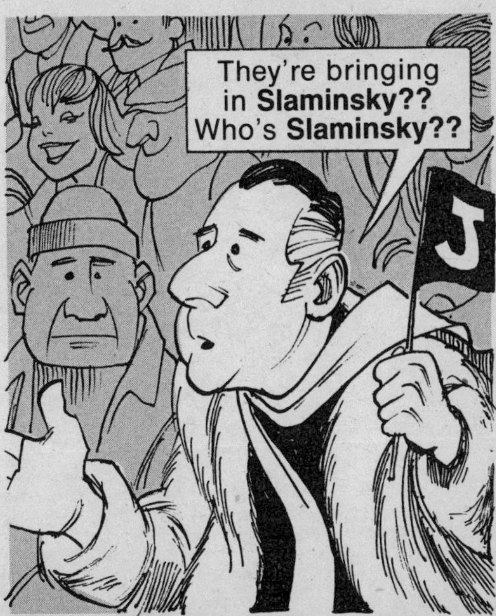
They're bringing in **Slaminsky??** Who's **Slaminsky??**

If Sportscasters Said What They'd Like To Say

WHAT THEY SAY

. . . and the Marmots, even though they're leading the Coyotes by 14 points, are going for a field goal with only seconds left in the game! It's clear Coach Gribbitz wants revenge for last season's humiliating loss to the Coyotes!

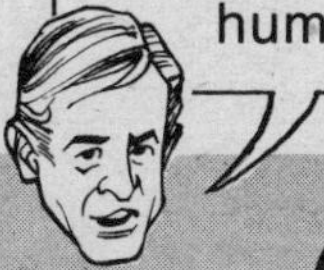

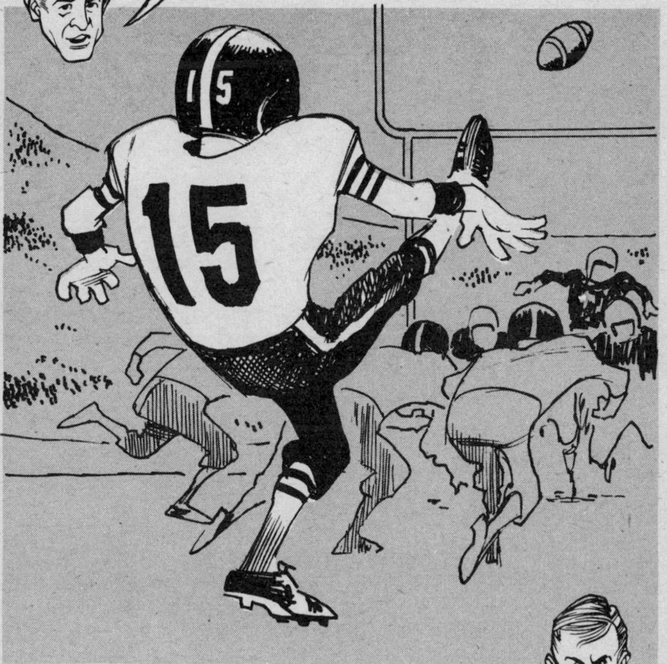

WHAT THEY'D LIKE TO SAY

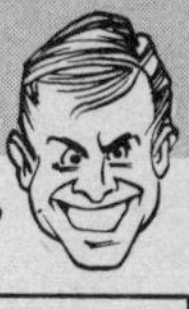

What revenge?! As usual, Gribbitz is only concerned with the **point-spread!** The Marmots are favored by 15, and unless they cover the spread, Gribbitz and his betting pals are going to lose a **ton of money!**

WHAT THEY SAY

. . . and here we are in the sixth inning, locked in an exciting scoreless pitchers duel! The two teams have combined for only five hits—an indication of the fine pitching we're seeing!

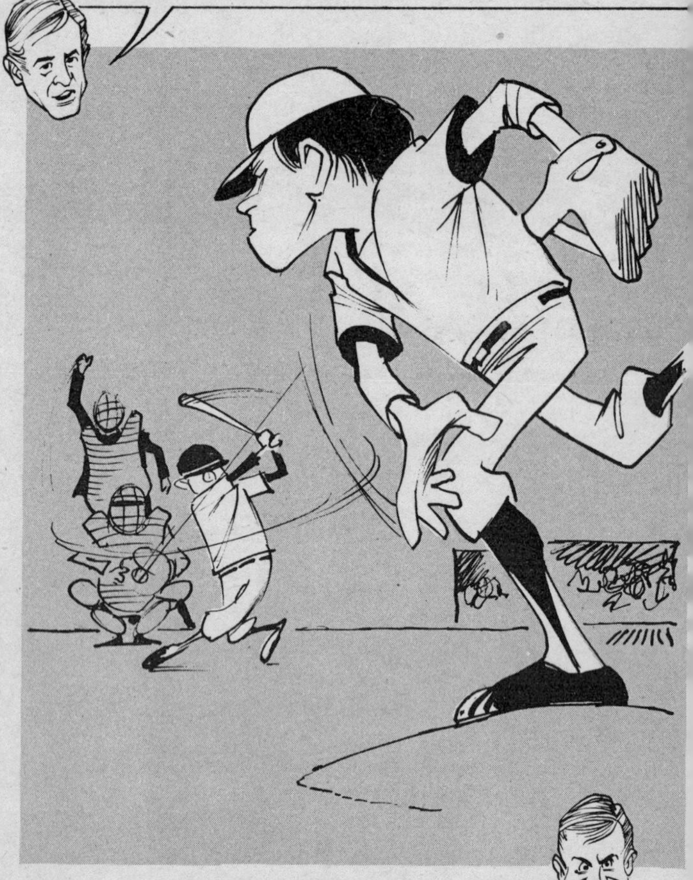

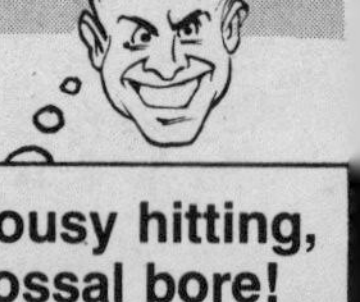

WHAT THEY'D LIKE TO SAY

But even more an indication of the **lousy hitting,** which makes this game such a **colossal bore!**

WHAT THEY SAY

. . . and Votz makes an incredible, tumbling catch, which is certainly the fielding play of the game!

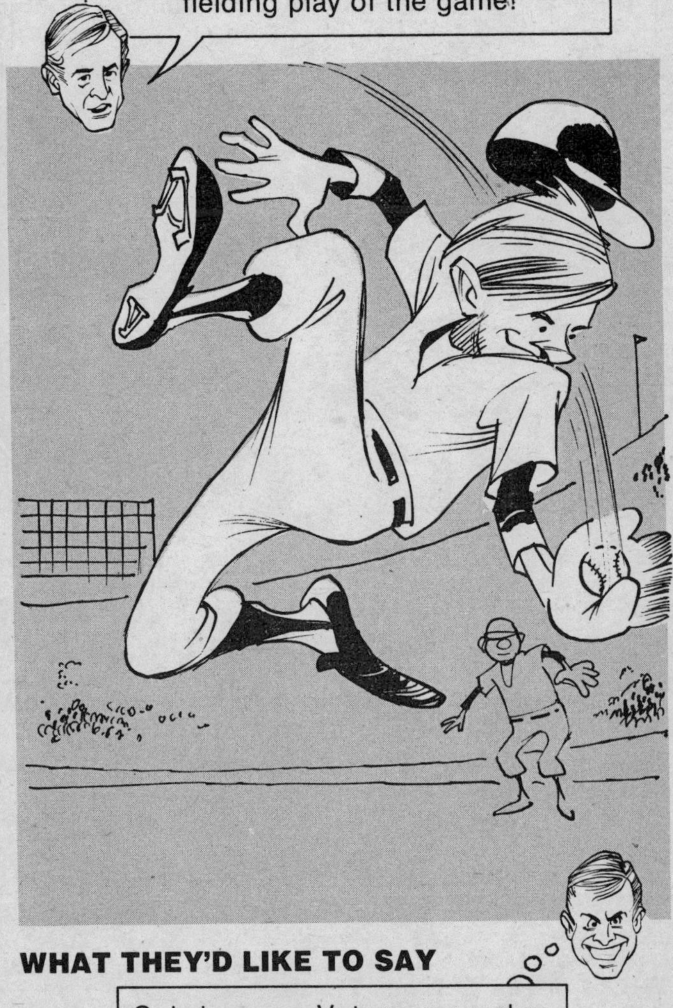

WHAT THEY'D LIKE TO SAY

Only because Votz **never** makes a catch look easy!

WHAT THEY SAY

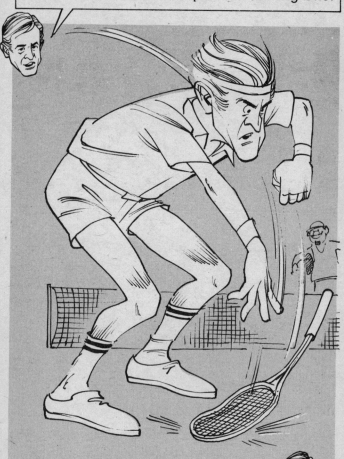

. . . and Culpepper double-faults, losing the tournament! A bitter loss for a great player who never seems able to pull out The Big One!

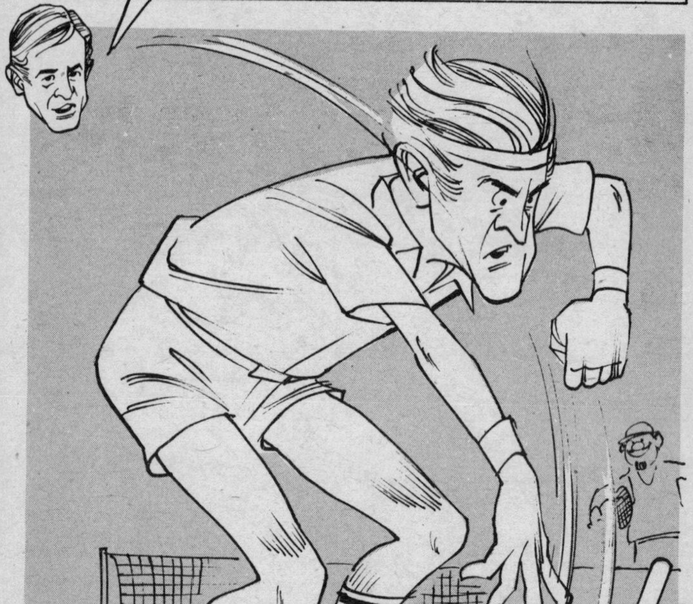

WHAT THEY'D LIKE TO SAY

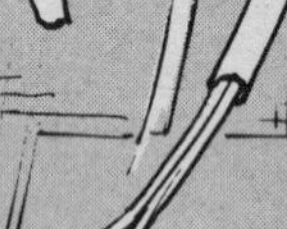

As usual, he **choked!**

WHAT THEY SAY

Froon is an unusual story! He never played Minor League ball and was a walk-on in Spring Training! And now he's the Dromedarys' new starting third baseman!

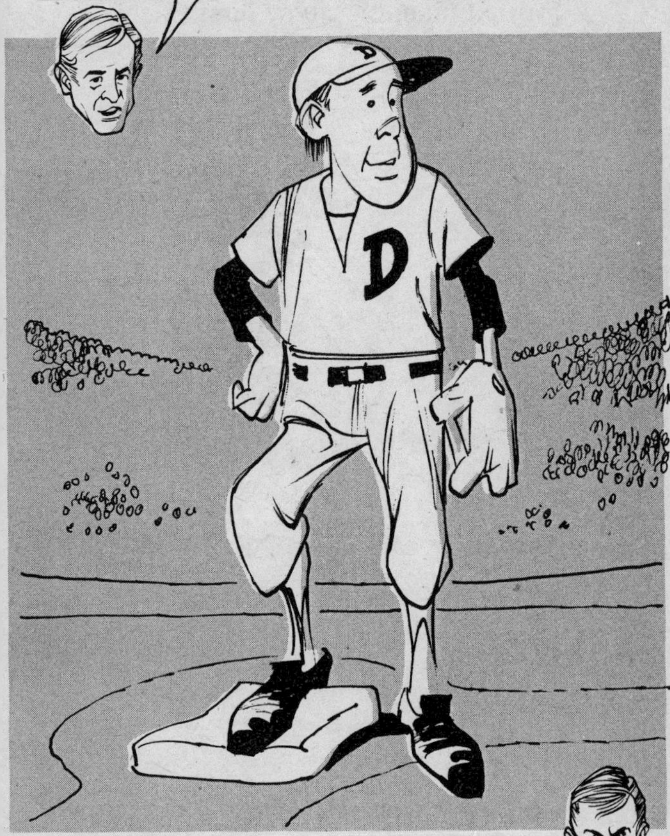
D
D

WHAT THEY'D LIKE TO SAY

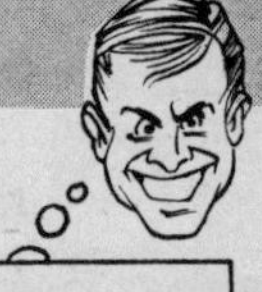

Which'll give you some small idea of how **rotten** the Dromedary farm system is!

WHAT THEY SAY

. . . and now Merkin and Sims, having wound up in a tie, begin their Sudden-Death Playoff! The winner will get $30,000 and the runner-up will pull down $18,000! So you can bet they'll be battling each other all the way for that nice, big, juicy First Prize!

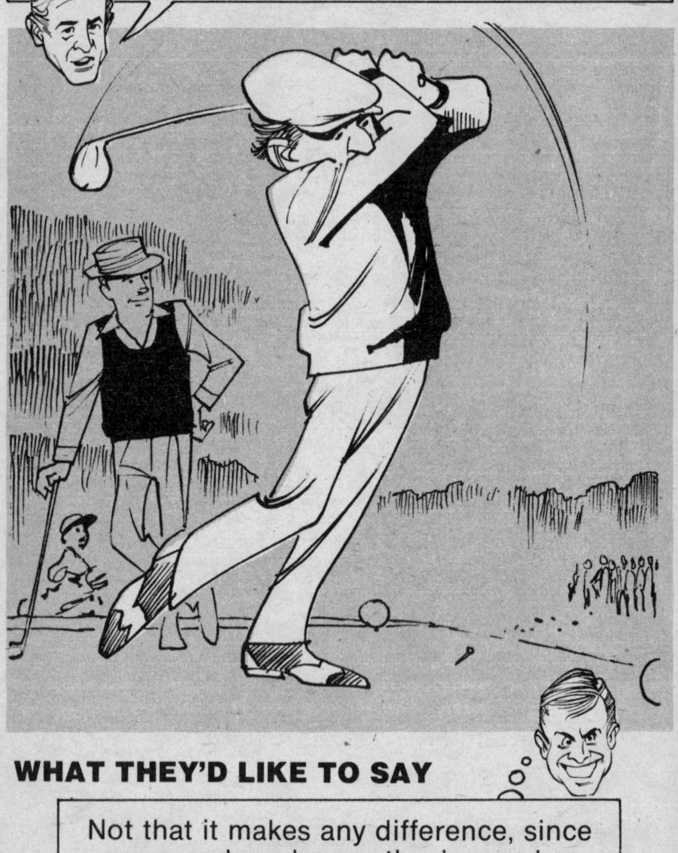

WHAT THEY'D LIKE TO SAY

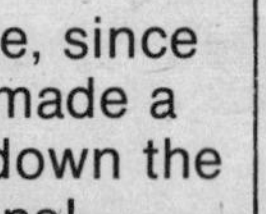

Not that it makes any difference, since everyone here knows they've made a **private deal** to split everything down the middle—no matter **who** wins!

WHAT THEY SAY

. . . and Smeegle crashes into the wall and now lies unconscious! A valiant effort!

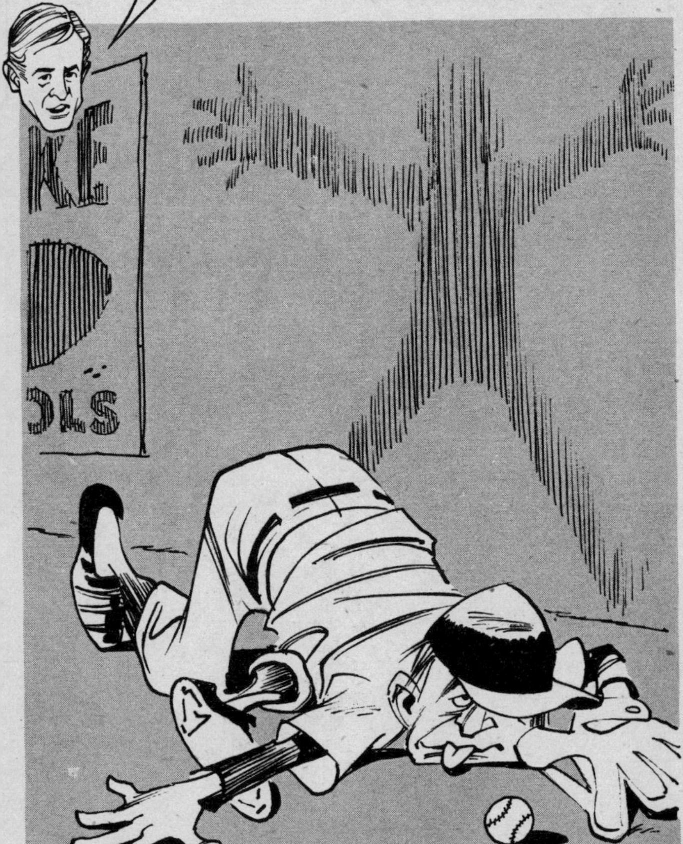

WHAT THEY'D LIKE TO SAY

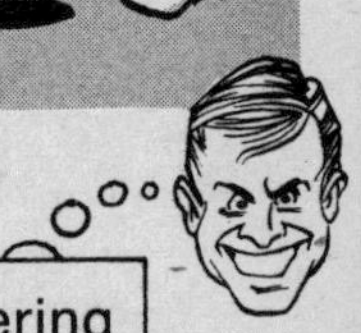

And a pretty **stupid** one, considering that his team is leading **15 to 1!**

WHAT THEY SAY

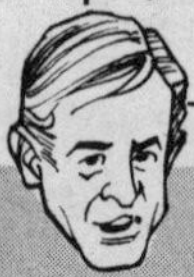

You've got to give Meefman points for courage— still hanging in there at the age of 38!

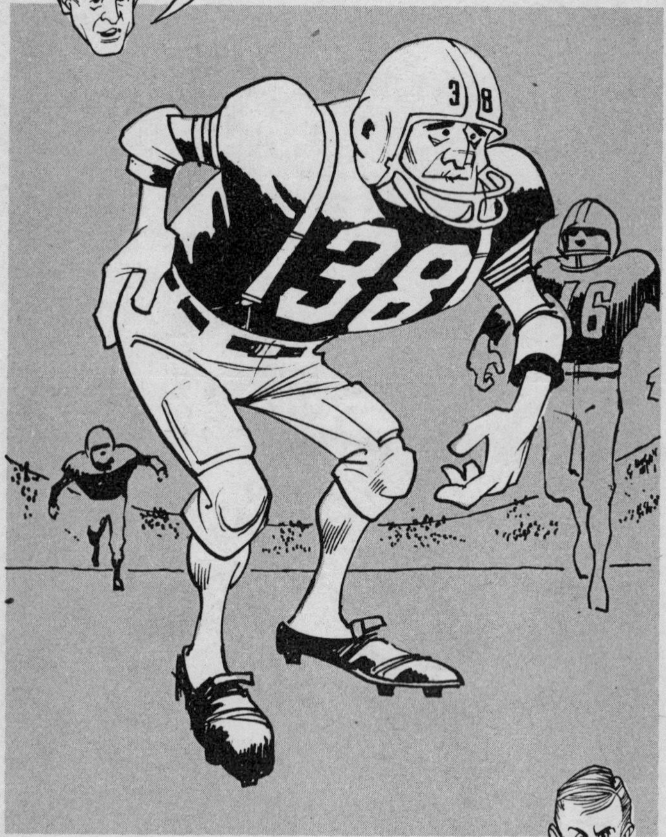

38

WHAT THEY'D LIKE TO SAY

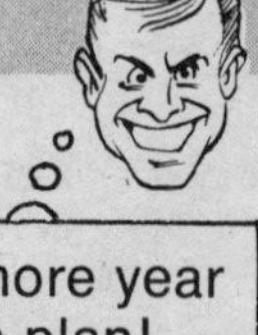

Why shouldn't he? He needs one more year to qualify for the league **pension** plan!

WHAT THEY SAY

Flotzam is an unselfish player! How many times have we seen him pass off to a teammate and let HIM make the basket?!

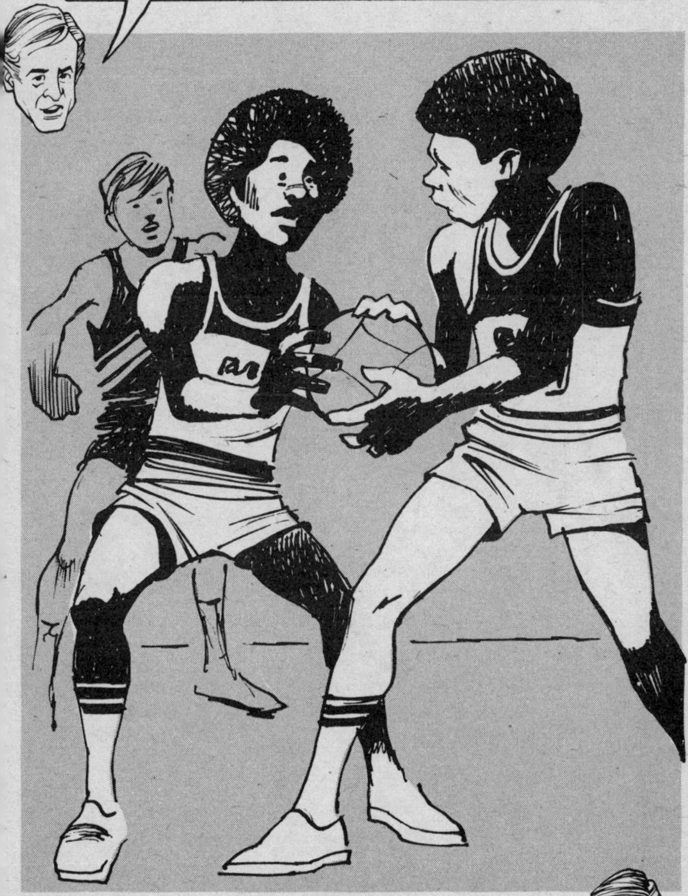

WHAT THEY'D LIKE TO SAY

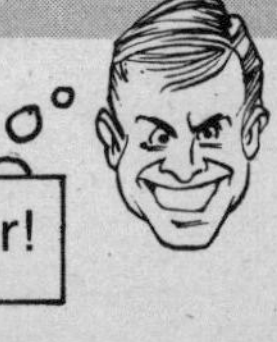

Flotzam **stinks** as a shooter!

WHAT THEY SAY

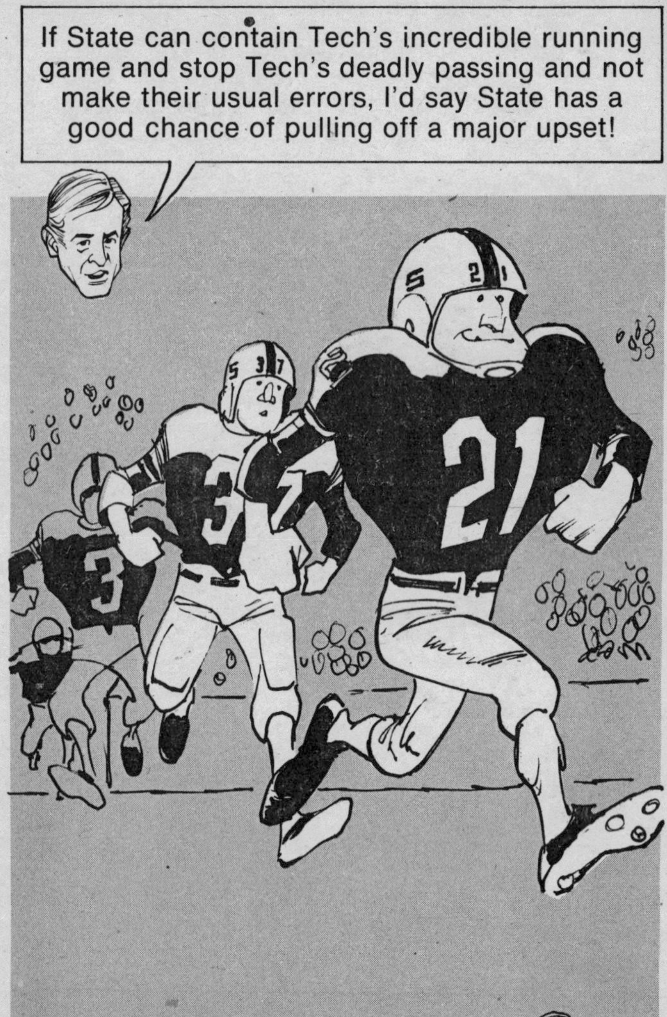
If State can contain Tech's incredible running game and stop Tech's deadly passing and not make their usual errors, I'd say State has a good chance of pulling off a major upset!

WHAT THEY'D LIKE TO SAY

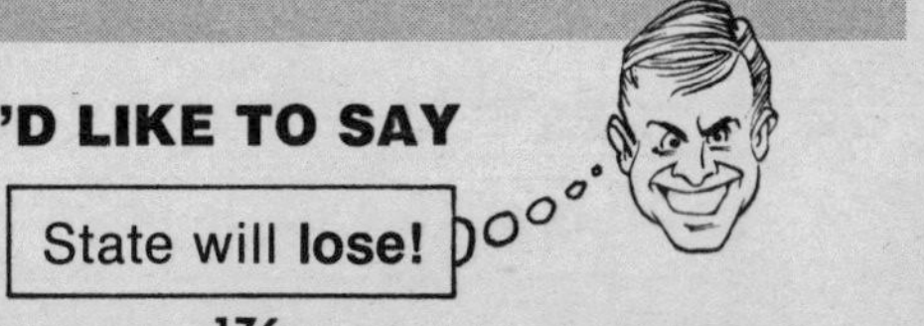
State will **lose!**

WHAT THEY SAY

The Rabbits come into this game a 17-point underdog! But having watched them in practice and seen their will to win, I really can't agree with that figure!

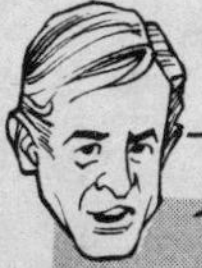

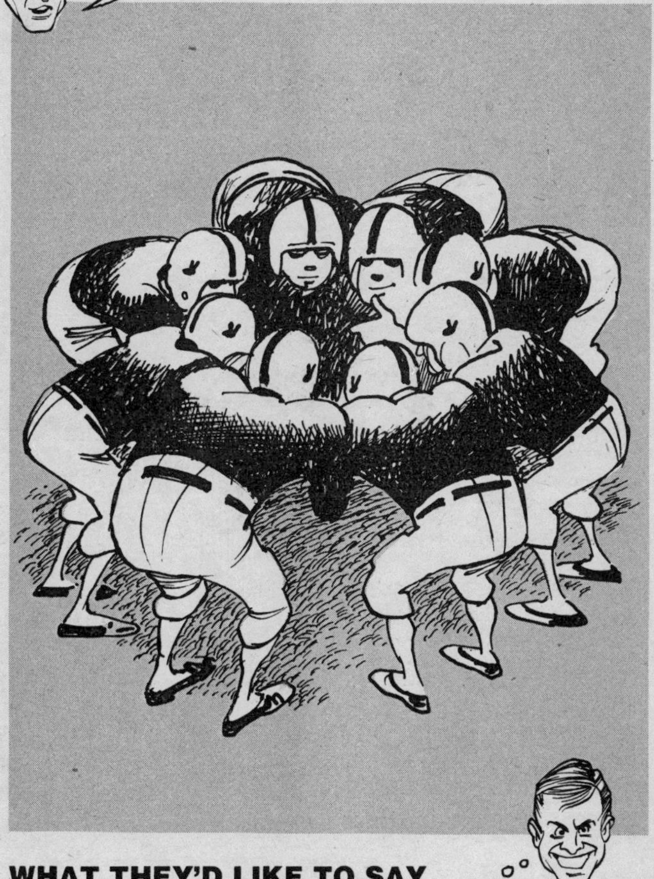

WHAT THEY'D LIKE TO SAY

They should be **35-point underdogs!**

WHAT THEY SAY

The woman in the hat is Lydia McCool, wife of starting pitcher Fox McCool! You can bet she's his Number One fan!

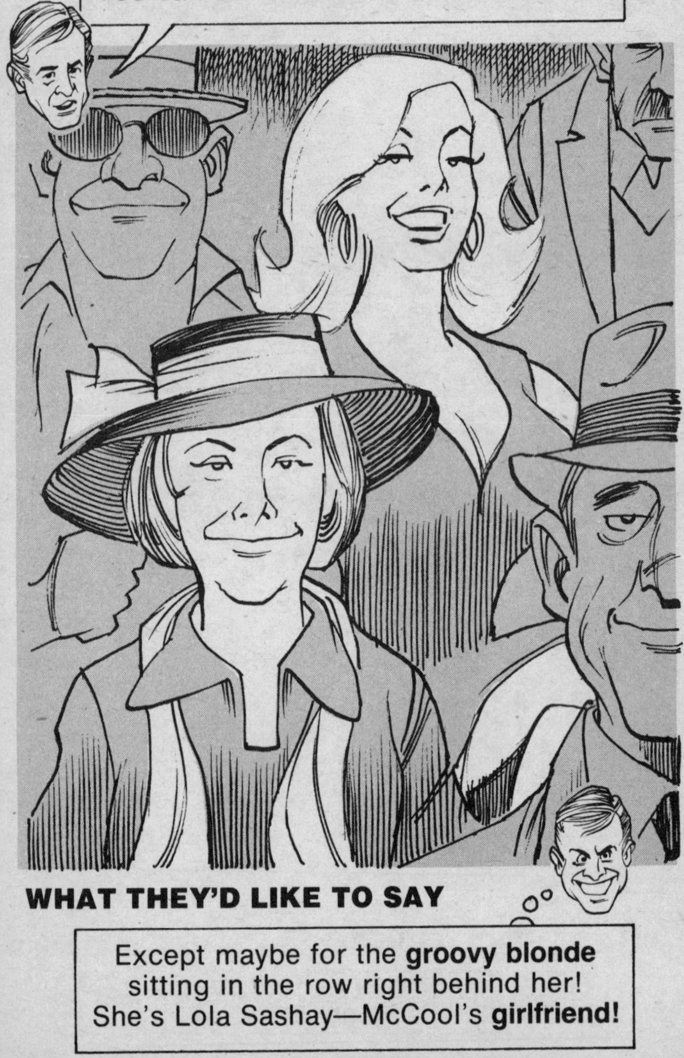

WHAT THEY'D LIKE TO SAY

Except maybe for the **groovy blonde** sitting in the row right behind her! She's Lola Sashay—McCool's **girlfriend!**

WHAT THEY SAY

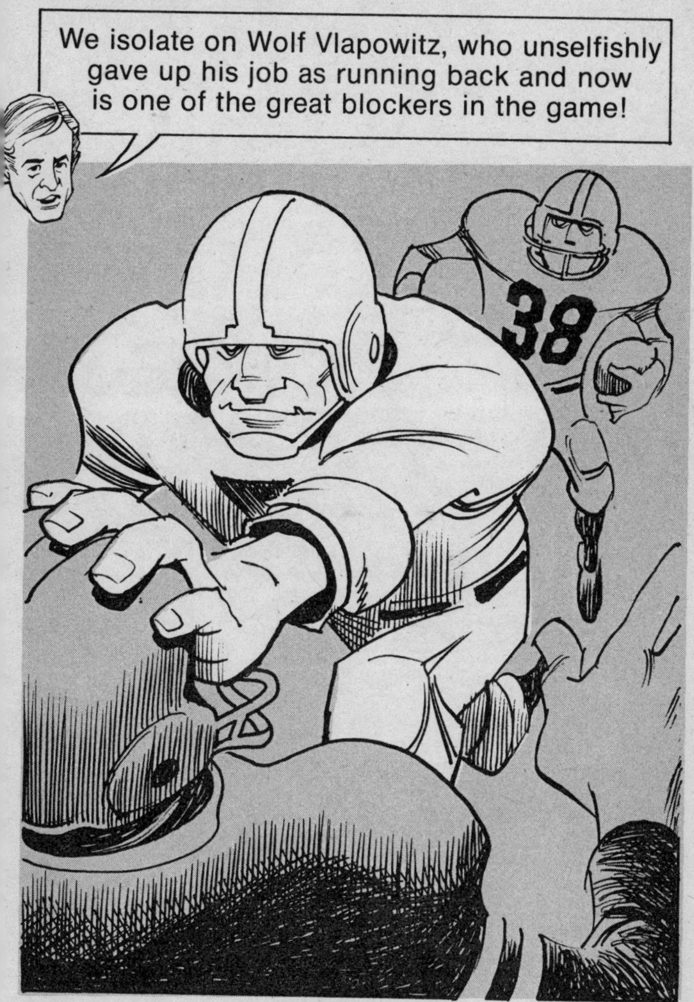
We isolate on Wolf Vlapowitz, who unselfishly gave up his job as running back and now is one of the great blockers in the game!
38

WHAT THEY'D LIKE TO SAY

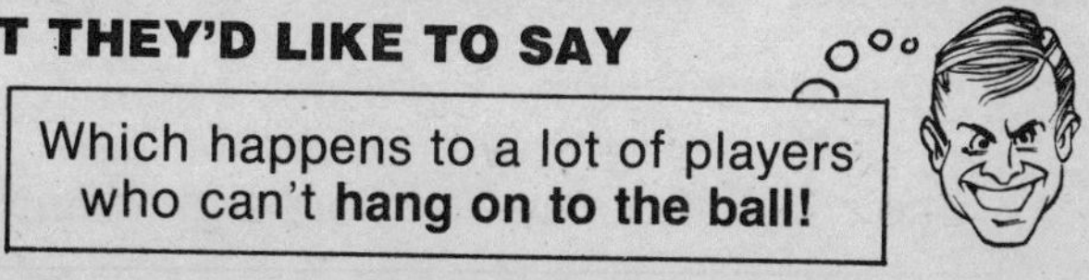
Which happens to a lot of players who can't **hang on to the ball!**

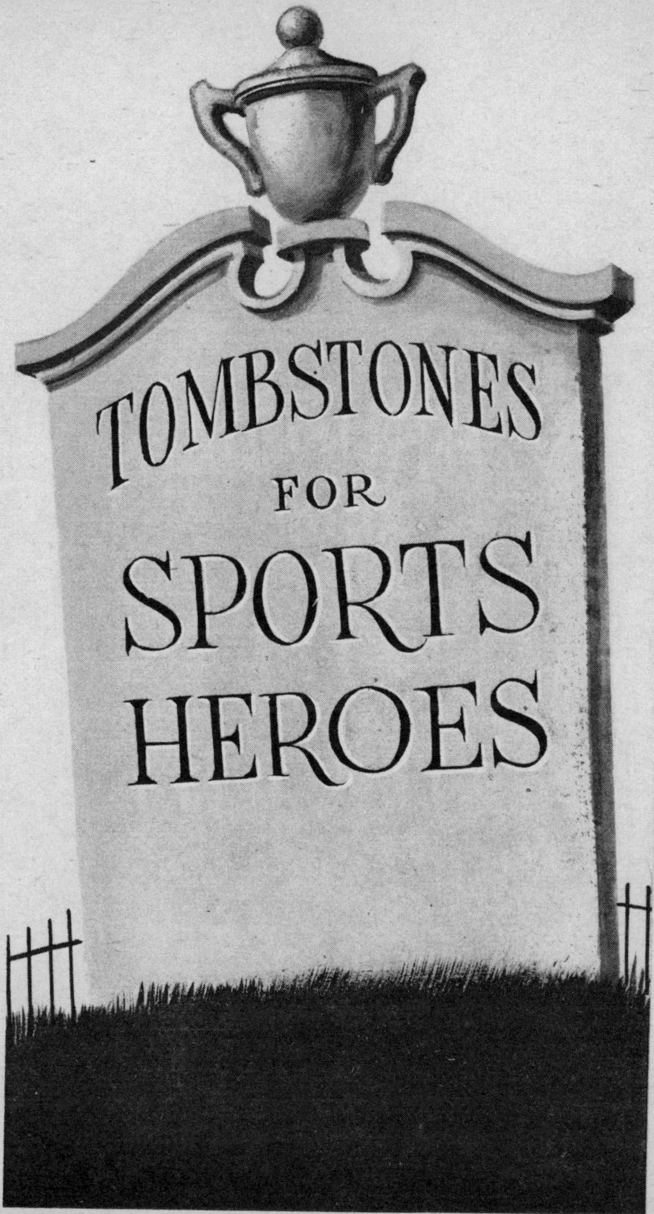
TOMBSTONES
FOR
SPORTS
HEROES

For a Football Player

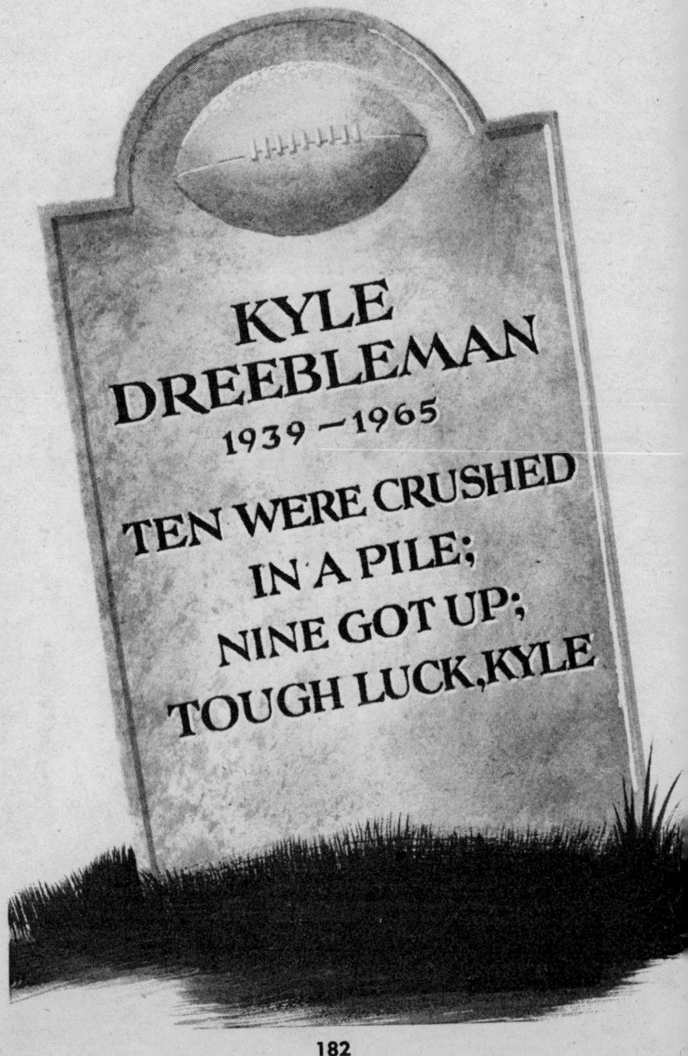

KYLE
DREEBLEMAN
1939 — 1965
TEN WERE CRUSHED
IN A PILE;
NINE GOT UP;
TOUGH LUCK, KYLE

For a Basketball Player

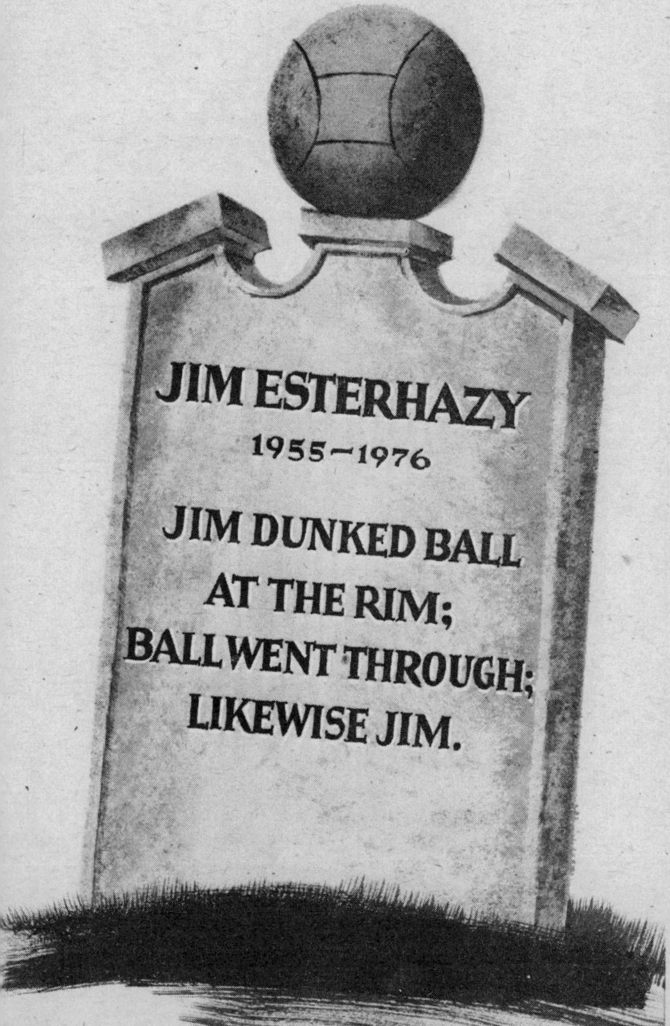
JIM ESTERHAZY
1955–1976
JIM DUNKED BALL
AT THE RIM;
BALL WENT THROUGH;
LIKEWISE JIM.

For a Hunter

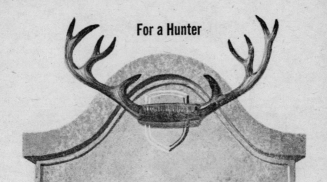

ROY
POINDEXTER
1932-1969

ROY AT LAST
UNDERSTANDS
GRIZZLY BEARS
DON'T SHAKE HANDS

For a Tennis Player

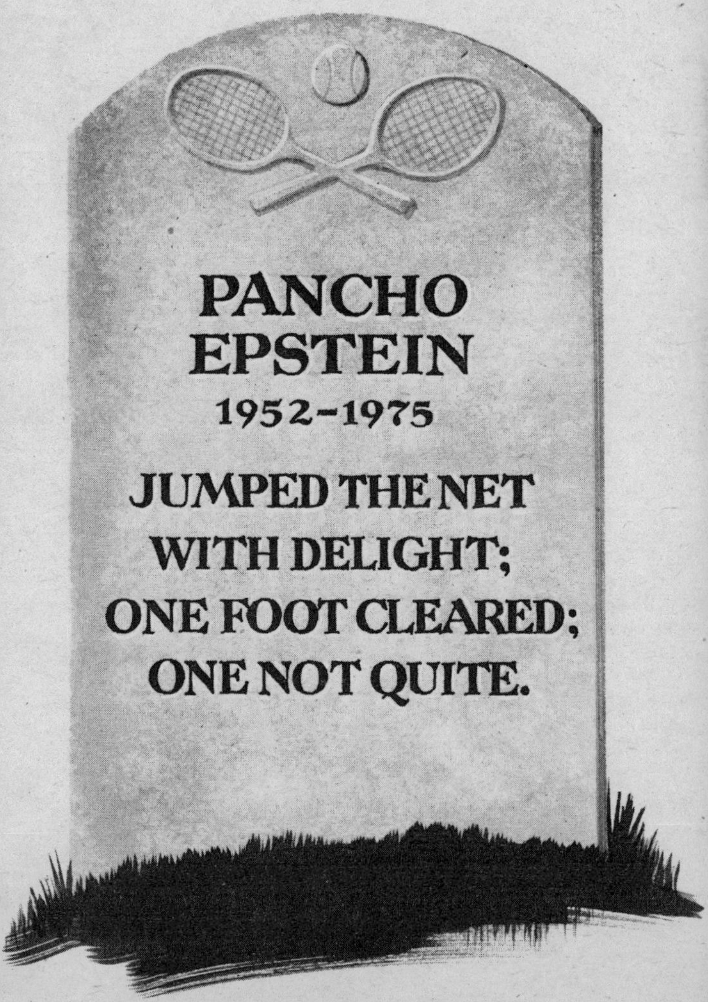
PANCHO
EPSTEIN
1952-1975
JUMPED THE NET
WITH DELIGHT;
ONE FOOT CLEARED;
ONE NOT QUITE.

For a Race-Car Driver

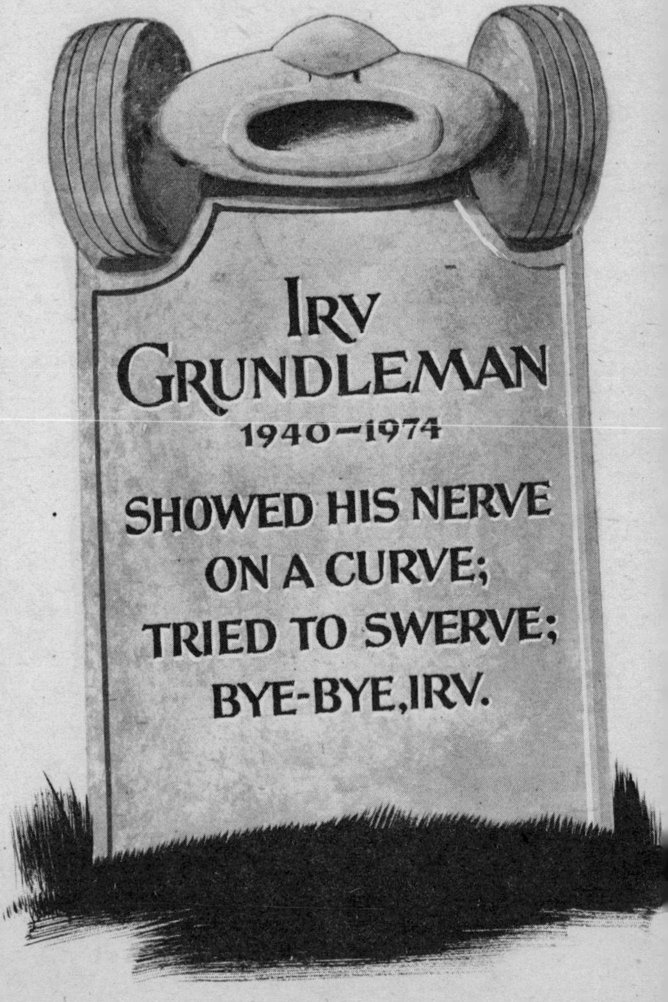
IRV GRUNDLEMAN
1940–1974
SHOWED HIS NERVE
ON A CURVE;
TRIED TO SWERVE;
BYE-BYE, IRV.

For a Jockey

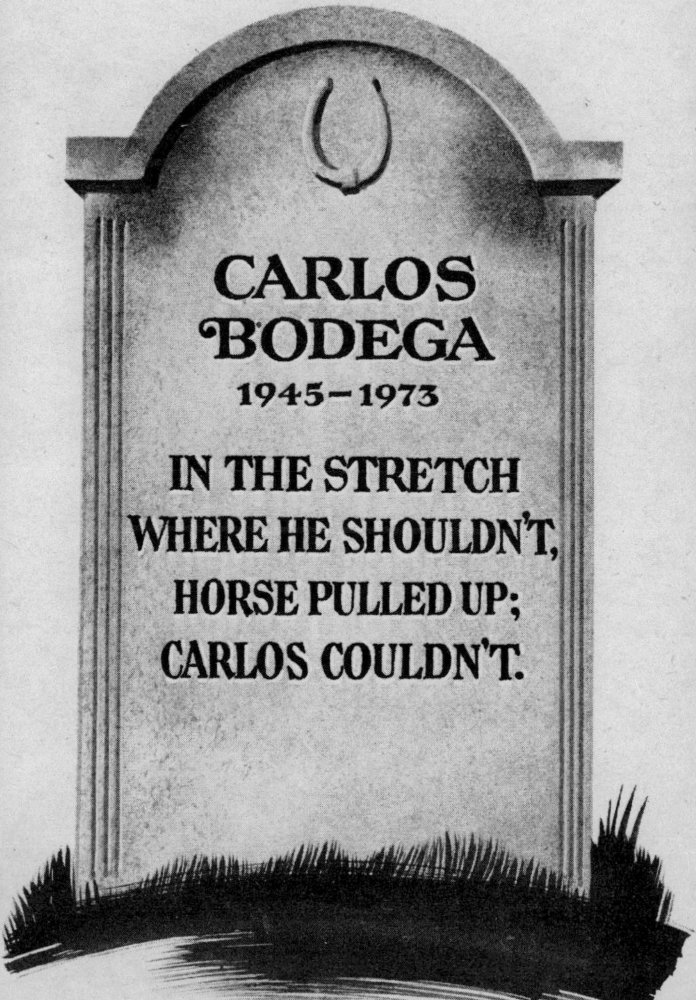
CARLOS
BODEGA
1945–1973
IN THE STRETCH
WHERE HE SHOULDN'T,
HORSE PULLED UP;
CARLOS COULDN'T.

For a Baseball Outfielder

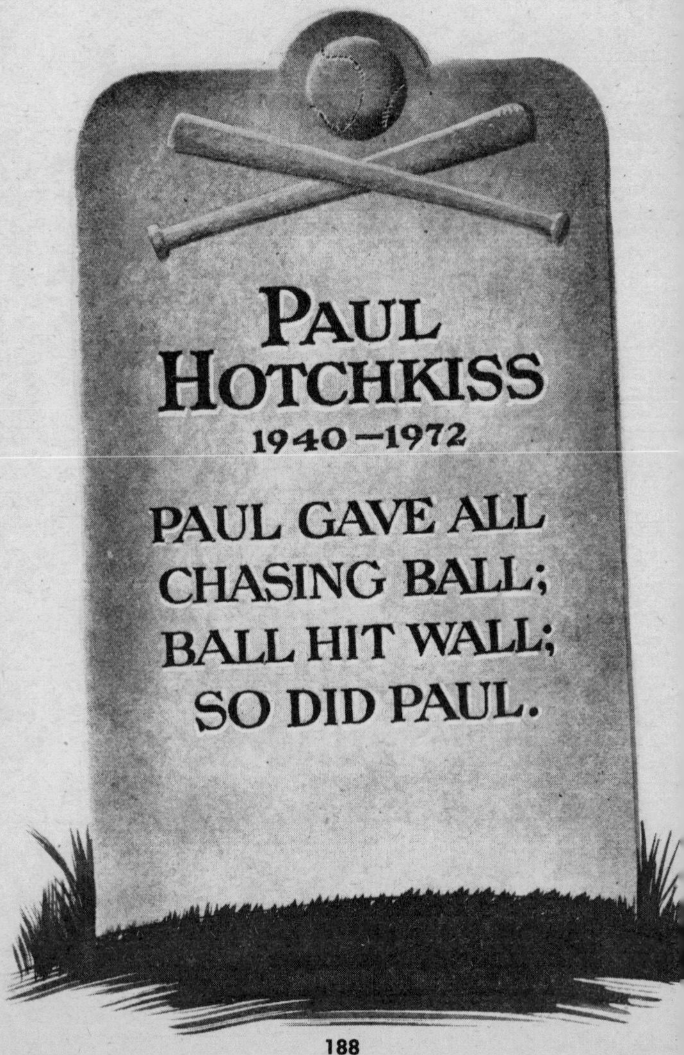
PAUL
HOTCHKISS
1940—1972
PAUL GAVE ALL
CHASING BALL;
BALL HIT WALL;
SO DID PAUL.

For a Bowler

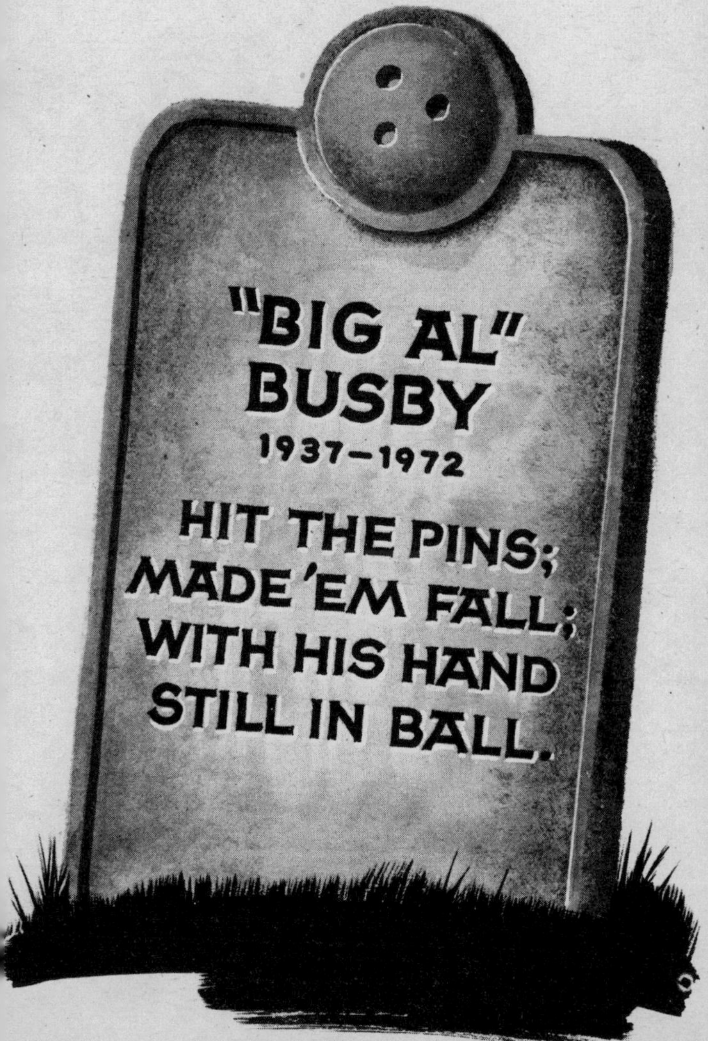
"BIG AL"
BUSBY
1937–1972
HIT THE PINS;
MADE 'EM FALL;
WITH HIS HAND
STILL IN BALL.

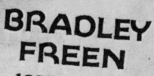

BRADLEY
FREEN
1955 — 1976

TOOK A DIVE
AFTER DARK;
LOST HIS SPEAR;
FOUND A SHARK.